LIGHTBULB MOMENTS *in* MARRIAGE

12 BIBLICAL PERSPECTIVES FOR SUCCESSFUL AND SATISFIED COUPLES

BIBLE STUDY GUIDE | SIX SESSIONS

EMERSON EGGERICHS PHD

Lightbulb Moments in Marriage Bible Study Guide

Published by HarperChristian Resources, 3950 Sparks Drive SE, Suite 101, Grand Rapids, MI 49546, USA. HarperChristian Resources is a registered trademark of HarperCollins Christian Publishing, Inc.

Requests for information should be sent to customercare@harpercollins.com.

ISBN 978-0-310-17897-2 (softcover)
ISBN 978-0-310-17898-9 (ebook)

HarperChristian Resources titles may be purchased in bulk for church, business, fundraising, or ministry use. For information, please e-mail ResourceSpecialist@ChurchSource.com.

Published in association with Punchline Agency.

HarperCollins Publishers, Macken House, 39/40 Mayor Street Upper, Dublin 1, D01 C9W8, Ireland (https://www.harpercollins.com).

Art Direction: Ron Huizinga
Cover Design: Meg Schmidt
Interior Design: Greg Jackson / Thinkpen Design

First Printing April 2026 / Printed in the United States of America

CONTENTS

Before You Begin: Emerson's Pastoral Coaching v

SESSION 1: OUR VALUE AND OUR INTENT

Lightbulb #1: God-Given, Not Spouse-Driven
Lightbulb #2: Seeing Jesus Beyond the Shoulder of Our Spouse

Group Session 1
Personal Study 9

Lightbulb #1: Biblical Foundation 10
Lightbulb #1: Practical Application 13
Lightbulb #2: Biblical Foundation 16
Lightbulb #2: Practical Application 19
Weekly Check-In 22

SESSION 2: OUR ETERNITY AND OUR WORLDVIEW

Lightbulb #3: Living with "Well Done!" in Mind
Lightbulb #4: The Holy Word, Not Hollywood

Group Session 25
Personal Study 33

Lightbulb #3: Biblical Foundation 34
Lightbulb #3: Practical Application 37
Lightbulb #4: Biblical Foundation 39
Lightbulb #4: Practical Application 42
Weekly Check-In 46

SESSION 3: OUR CLARITY AND OUR HARMONY

Lightbulb #5: Understanding Each Other, Not Just Talking
Lightbulb #6: Same Team, Same Goal, Different Plays

Group Session 49
Personal Study 57

Lightbulb #5: Biblical Foundation 58
Lightbulb #5: Practical Application 64
Lightbulb #6: Biblical Foundation 68
Lightbulb #6: Practical Application 74
Weekly Check-In 79

SESSION 4: OUR ACKNOWLEDGMENT AND OUR TENSION

Lightbulb #7: Not Wrong, Just Different Shades of Right
Lightbulb #8: Don't Let the 20% Define the 80%

Group Session 81
Personal Study 89

Lightbulb #7: Biblical Foundation 90
Lightbulb #7: Practical Application 93
Lightbulb #8: Biblical Foundation 96
Lightbulb #8: Practical Application 99
Weekly Check-In 103

SESSION 5: OUR SELF-AWARENESS AND OUR AUTHENTICITY

Lightbulb #9: When I Get Defensive, Do I Get Offensive Too?
Lightbulb #10: Motivation Without Manipulation

Group Session 105
Personal Study 113

Lightbulb #9: Biblical Foundation 114
Lightbulb #9: Practical Application 117
Lightbulb #10: Biblical Foundation 120
Lightbulb #10: Practical Application 123
Weekly Check-In 125

SESSION 6: OUR FORGIVENESS AND OUR EMPOWERMENT

Lightbulb #11: Not Offending—Just Misunderstood
Lightbulb #12: Free and Strong When I Live Out, "My Response Is My Responsibility"

Group Session 127
Personal Study 133

Lightbulb #11: Biblical Foundation 134
Lightbulb #11: Practical Application 137
Lightbulb #12: Biblical Foundation 141
Lightbulb #12: Practical Application 143
Weekly Check-In 146

About the Author 147

BEFORE YOU BEGIN

EMERSON'S PASTORAL COACHING

One *lightbulb moment* can change everything about your marriage. These are those moments when the "lightbulb" goes on in your head and you suddenly have an illuminating insight. These are the kinds of truths that, once grasped, you can't unsee:

My parents aren't perfect.
Honest is the best policy.
Failure isn't the end but the beginning.

In this study, your group will meet for 75 to 125 minutes to discuss the *Lightbulb Moments in Marriage* message. Sharing in a small group can feel vulnerable. You may wonder what to say or whether opening up will make things worse. I understand. That's why I want to invite you into a gentler way of relating during this study.

This time is not about fixing your marriage or proving a point. It is about paying attention to what God is doing in *you*. These conversations are meant to strengthen trust, not diagnose everything that's wrong. Let's keep things simple, safe, and Spirit-led.

Helpful Guidelines

1. Speak only for yourself. Share what encouraged or challenged *you*, not what you think your spouse needs to do.
2. Resist correcting or lecturing. This is not the moment to "teach" your spouse through your comments.
3. Use "I" statements, such as:

    "I realized something about myself . . ."
    "I sensed God encouraging me here . . ."
    "This truth made me rethink my reactions . . ."

4. Let grace lead. If your spouse shares imperfectly, appreciate the effort rather than critique the wording.
5. Stay on topic. Focus on what stood out from the video or workbook.
6. Remember the purpose: to share how God is speaking to *your* heart, not to work through every layer of pain.

Goal for Husbands and Wives: Sharing Personal Encouragement

During the group time (and again during your Weekly Check-In), take a few quiet minutes to share what personally encouraged you. For example:

> "Here's what spoke to my heart this week. I was encouraged to remember that my worth is God-given. I needed that reminder."
>
> What this time is *not*:
>
> "As I engaged the content, I realized how far we still have to go and how you keep avoiding the real issues."

That type of comment may feel true but it shuts things down. This study is about "aha" moments—not ammunition. Keep it positive, personal, and focused on what God is revealing in you.

Understanding the Differences in What Encourages

The most satisfied couples are not those who process life the same way but those who honor each other's differences. Equality does not mean sameness.

A wife may long for her husband to express something she considers profound and feel disappointed when he doesn't. A husband may wait for his wife to "finally get it" and feel confused when her encouragement seems unrelated to his concerns.

Let me gently remind you: What matters in these moments is honesty and humility about how God is working in *your* heart.

When Feeling Put Down or Ignored

Men and women often communicate differently, and sometimes a comment may land wrong. When something feels hurtful, pause before reacting. Ask yourself, *Have I understood their heart correctly?* Then ask your spouse, "Can you help me understand what you meant?"

Clarity softens what assumptions harden. If a comment feels like finger-pointing, stay calm. Seek to follow the guidelines and recognize occasional missteps are simply part of being human. Resist the urge to declare, "This study isn't helping." That only deepens the divide.

If you feel criticized, guard your spirit. Stay quiet for the moment. Choose not to take up an offense. Trust the process. In the long term, this study will bring life if you stay focused on what God is doing in you.

Sometimes the wisest question you can ask yourself is, *Should I say this now, or should I stay positive in this moment?*

Remember how Jesus framed marriage in Matthew 19:4: God made us male and female. Not wrong, just different.

When Men Go Quiet

Men don't always grow silent because they don't care. Often they care deeply. Many men:

- Pull back from long, intense conversations
- Experience emotional "flooding"
- Re-engage best when the tone feels respectful and purposeful

Silence isn't always withdrawal. Sometimes it means, "I don't want to fail you, so I'm being cautious." That is why low-pressure questions during Weekly Check-In times can help:

- "What encouraged you this week?"
- "Was there something that gave you a new perspective?"

These gentle invitations help husbands open up without feeling examined or corrected.

This isn't about avoiding important issues. It's about creating the kind of atmosphere where a husband can stay engaged, not overwhelmed.

When Women Speak Up

Women often seek connection through words. They carry emotional memory vividly and may speak in order to feel close again. Her heart often says, "Do I still matter to you?"

If the husband hears only critique, he may withdraw, which triggers her further. She pushes for closeness, he steps back, and both feel misunderstood.

Some wives, however, are quieter and need encouragement to share honestly. Some husbands are verbal but use words to explain rather than connect, which can sound like defensiveness.

Whatever your pattern, growth begins with owning your part rather than correcting your spouse's.

Expect Tension—It Often Leads to Breakthrough

Two people who have shared life for years will occasionally feel old frustrations stirred. That does not mean something is failing. Scripture and research agree that transformation often happens under pressure. Tension can lead to:

- Replacing a harmful belief with God's truth
- A shift from demanding love to offering love

- Understanding a spouse's fear rather than assuming the worst
- Seeing your own blind spot clearly for the first time

These moments are often sacred ground. The places that feel overwhelming may become the very lightbulb moments God uses to soften hearts, increase empathy, and deepen trust.

If You're Stuck

If bitterness is rising, reach out to someone. God often brings help through others. A simple coffee conversation with another couple may become a turning point.

Concrete Ways to Build Understanding

For husbands:

- Pause and ask, "Is she pursuing me, not pressuring me?"
- Affirm her intent.
- Ask for clarity.
- Offer vulnerability: "Help me say this well."

For wives:

- Affirm his effort.
- Give him space to process.
- Invite openness with gentle curiosity.
- Speak with grace: "Help me express this respectfully."

A Shared Goal

You both want to feel seen, understood, and valued.

He needs to know you believe in his deepest heart.

She needs to know her heart matters more than any solution.

You are not opponents. You are a team. You may feel differently about the same moment and still both be right—just different shades of right.

You do not need perfection. You need willingness. Willingness to try, to listen, and to reconnect even when it's hard.

Get Ready for the Stumbles

A wife may begin hopeful, only to feel stung by something he says without meaning harm. A husband may begin trying earnestly, only to feel defeated by her reaction. Each waits to be understood rather than seeking to understand. This is where small shifts matter.

One phrase can change everything:

"I want to better understand what you think and feel. Can you help me?"

That mindset reopens hearts. It restores closeness.
It turns tension into transformation.

What to Expect

Small Group Time Commitment

Total Time Range: One hour and fifteen minutes on the short end and around two hours on the longer end. This format provides structure while leaving room for meaningful conversations, laughter, prayer, and connection. The flow is designed to be life-giving—not rushed.

Typical Weekly Breakdown

Segment	Time Range	Description
Welcome and Connect	5–15 minutes	Informal check-in, light conversation, and a simple "Connect" question or two to open hearts.
Watch the Video	30–40 minutes	Watch the video session together—each week includes two Lightbulb Moments per video.
Group Discussion	30–45 minutes	Reflect on the video using the discussion guide. Emphasize encouragement, insight, and personal testimony—not spouse critique.
Husband and Wife Time	5–15 minutes	A few minutes for each couple to share privately about "what encouraged me," using a guided format.
Group Prayer	5–10 minutes	A short time of prayer or blessing to close. Group members may take turns leading or follow a written prayer.
TOTAL	75–125 minutes	Adjust flexibly based on group size and dynamic. Shorter if focused and intimate; longer if the group is more conversational.

Personal Study (at Home)

There are two approaches you can take (and it's okay to choose what works best). *Give your spouse the freedom to choose their preference. You don't have to match!*

1. Choose Your Adventure (approximately fifteen minutes total): Select *one* insight from the **Biblical Foundation** section and *one* action from the **Practical Application** to focus on during the week.

2. Full Study (approximately 2 hours total): Read and reflect on all the content in the **Biblical Foundation** and **Practical Application** sections related to both Lightbulb Moments.

Weekly Spouse Check-In (at Home)

Suggested Time: Fifteen minutes

Each week, you and your spouse will set aside time to discuss:

- What encouraged you in the session . . .
- What God is doing in you, not what needs fixing in your spouse.

NOT JUST
MORE EFFORT
BUT MORE LIGHT.
SMALL LIGHTBULB MOMENTS.
SMALL STEPS.
BIG DIFFERENCE.

BEFORE GROUP MEETING	Read the introduction and chapters 1–2 in *Lightbulb Moments in Marriage* Read the Welcome section (pages 2–3)
GROUP MEETING	Discuss the Connect questions (page 3) Watch the video teaching for session 1 and take notes (pages 4–6) Engage in a Group Discussion on the material (page 7) Couples have a Husband and Wife Discussion (pages 7–8) Close in Group Prayer (page 8)
PERSONAL STUDY	
LIGHTBULB MOMENT #1: BIBLICAL FOUNDATION	Complete the Biblical Foundation personal study for Lightbulb Moment #1 (pages 10–12)
LIGHTBULB MOMENT #1: PRACTICAL APPLICATION	Complete the Practical Application personal study for Lightbulb Moment #1 (pages 13–15)
LIGHTBULB MOMENT #2: BIBLICAL FOUNDATION	Complete the Biblical Foundation personal study for Lightbulb Moment #2 (pages 16–18)
LIGHTBULB MOMENT #2: PRACTICAL APPLICATION	Complete the Practical Application personal study for Lightbulb Moment #2 (pages 19–21)
WEEKLY CHECK-IN	Connect with your spouse during the week to discuss your key insights from this session (pages 22–23)
BEFORE NEXT WEEK	Read chapters 3–4 in *Lightbulb Moments in Marriage*

SESSION ONE

OUR VALUE AND OUR INTENT

LIGHTBULB #1:

God-Given, Not Spouse-Driven

Your worth doesn't rise or fall with your spouse's moods, opinions, or actions—God gave you value because of Jesus. That settles it.

LIGHTBULB #2:

Seeing Jesus Beyond the Shoulder of Our Spouse

How you treat your spouse moves the heart of Christ. He invites you to look beyond them to Him—loving and reverencing Him in a way that naturally overflows onto your spouse.

Welcome [READ ON YOUR OWN]

Marriage often reveals our most beautiful strengths and our deepest vulnerabilities.

Many husbands quietly carry the weight of not feeling good enough. They long to be respected and valued, especially in conflict. Many wives crave to feel cherished and emotionally connected, and feel hurt when their pain is met with silence instead of empathy.

Both want connection. Both long to feel prized. But too often, they miss each other in the trying. We know those moments:

- You give love, but it seems unnoticed.
- You show respect, but it's dismissed.
- You reach for closeness and feel pushed away.

These moments impact more than emotions. They touch our identity. And that's where this study begins. Maybe you're feeling this right now:

- Wives thinking, "He should be cherishing me, but I feel unseen."
- Husbands feeling, "She's too critical. I'll never be enough."

These feelings are real. They matter. And you are not alone. You are not a failure.

Sarah and I have been married since 1973. And even now, we still encounter moments of hurt, miscommunication, and unmet expectations. But here's the hope: God is not absent in those moments. In fact, He may be most active there.

Secular research affirms what Scripture has always revealed: It's often in relational struggle that our deepest growth occurs. Neuroscience shows that meaningful transformation is more likely during seasons of stress and emotional discomfort, when the brain is actively re-evaluating patterns and seeking new responses. Psychologists call this *transformational learning* or *cognitive restructuring*. This is a shift in thinking that changes how we see ourselves, others, and the future. A lightbulb moment, if you will.

So when tension rises in marriage, it's not just a disruption to avoid. It's an opportunity. An invitation. A holy moment in disguise.

God uses even the painful parts of marriage not to break us, but to make us more like Christ. Not to punish, but to purify. He's not only building a better relationship. He's building something eternal in you.

These moments are not just about you and your spouse. They're about your faith.

The first few chapters of *Lightbulb Moments in Marriage* focus on how we respond not just to each other, but to God in our marriage. In this first session, reflecting chapters one and two, we ask: *Will I trust who God says I am? Will I see Him standing just beyond the shoulder of my spouse?*

This is the upward dimension of marriage. It's not only about "How do I respond to my spouse?" but, "How do I respond to God in this moment?"

God wants to enlighten you, even when your spouse doesn't change. Whether your marriage is thriving or struggling, this study offers two core truths to anchor your soul.

Lightbulb Moment #1 is about our value: *God-Given, Not Spouse-Driven*. Even if your spouse is unresponsive, inattentive, or hurtful, your value is unchanged. We will consider this simple but profound truth: "God created man in His own image . . ." (Genesis 1:27 NASB).

You will be reminded, as Christ followers, that your worth isn't determined by your spouse's image of you but by God's image of you. You are made in His image. Thus, as important as your spouse's words or actions are, they do not determine God's view of you. It's been set by God Himself, secured in Christ, and is unshakeable.

When you feel unseen, God sees. When your heart aches, He cares. As one person said, "The Father of Jesus is fond of me." This truth doesn't dismiss your pain; it roots you in something deeper than your circumstances.

So here's the question: *When my spouse's reactions unsettle me, will I let that define me, or will I return to the One who already declared my worth?*

Lightbulb Moment #2 is about our intent: *Seeing Jesus Beyond the Shoulder of Our Spouse*. When your spouse seems indifferent to the love or respect you offer, it's tempting to stop trying.

But it always matters to Jesus. Every time you love in difficulty or respect without reward, you touch the heart of Christ Himself.

Marriage becomes both a tool and a test, not just of your relationship, but of your love and reverence for Him.

Picture Jesus standing just beyond your spouse's shoulder. Not judging but smiling. Watching. Whispering, "That matters to Me. You matter to Me."

So let me ask: *Is your heart moved by how God sees you? Do you believe you move His heart, even when your spouse doesn't respond?*

That's what we'll explore together, individually, as couples, and as a group.

Let's invite God to speak fresh truth into how we see ourselves, our spouse, and most of all, the Lord Himself.

Connect [5 TO 15 MINUTES]

If you or any of the other couples in your group don't know each other, take a few minutes to introduce yourselves. Then discuss one or both of the following questions:

- Why did you decide to participate in this study?

— *or* —

- As you read the Welcome section, was there a phrase or idea that made you think, *Yes, that's what I need to hear more about*? What question did that stir in you?

Watch [30 TO 40 MINUTES]

Watch the video teaching as a group, which you can access through streaming (see the instructions provided with this guide). Below is an outline of the session to follow along. Feel free to underline what stands out.

Outline: Lightbulb Moments #1 & #2

I. What Are Lightbulb Moments in Marriage?

- Sudden, clarifying insights . . . moments when something finally *clicks*.
- Like childhood realizations ("My parents aren't perfect"), these insights can pivot a marriage in a powerful way.
- In this study, we explore twelve biblical lightbulb moments that help couples grow in identity, connection, and emotional intelligence.

II. Lightbulb Moment #1—Our Value: God-Given, Not Spouse-Driven

- Your value doesn't rise or fall with your spouse's behavior or approval.
- We must bring our identity in Christ into the marriage, not get it from the marriage.
- I share personal stories from my early Christian life, where I discovered God's incredible love and forgiveness.
- My faith in Jesus began at military school after watching the Billy Graham film *For Pete's Sake*. However, after entering Wheaton College, I felt deeply inadequate as a new believer surrounded by impressive peers.
- At a freshman retreat, chaplain Evan Welsh overwhelmed me with a holy compassion I had never experienced from anyone when he gently rebuked me: "Don't you ever say I love people more than you. You will love far more than I ever will."
- Later, God used that episode when I struggled with His love for me. The Lord whispered to my heart: *If Evan Welsh, a mere man, could love you, would I love you less?* This became a defining lightbulb moment.
- During that time, Dr. Gordon Fee shared a story of a believer confessing sin to Jesus, saying, "Lord, I've sinned again. Will You forgive me again?" And Jesus replied, "Again? I don't recall the last time." That picture of divine forgiveness was an "aha" moment for me.
- Months later, while leading a youth group, I shared what I had just learned and said, "If you were the only person alive, Jesus would have come and died for you." A thirteen-year-old boy responded: "Yeah, and you'd be the one who crucified Him." That insight cut me to the heart and deepened my understanding of what I meant to Jesus.
- These moments, early in my faith, not only stunned me and caused major paradigm shifts but also positively impacted how I did marriage later.

Key Metaphors:

- When your identity hinges on your spouse's opinion, everyday interactions begin to feel like a trial. Their mood becomes the jury, their words the verdict. One smile acquits you, one frown condemns you. But God has already rendered the final ruling at the cross: fully loved, eternally accepted.
- Your worth is not something your spouse was meant to author. That pen belongs to God alone. When you hand them the pen, you risk letting their wounds, silence, or criticism rewrite what Christ already declared about you. You are priceless, not because your spouse says so, but because God already did.

Key Scriptures:

- 1 Corinthians 1:8: You are blameless in Christ.
- 1 Corinthians 6:20: You were bought with a price.
- Romans 8:1: No condemnation in Christ.
- Romans 8:17: You're a co-heir with Christ.
- 1 John 3:1: You're a deeply loved child of God.

Key Takeaways:

- You are worth Jesus to the Father.
- You are not defined by your spouse's reaction but by God's declaration.
- If you let a wounded spouse define your worth, you live wounded too.
- Your identity must rest in Christ or you'll always feel on trial in your marriage.

III. Lightbulb Moment #2—Our Intent: Seeing Jesus Beyond the Shoulder of Our Spouse

- Marriage becomes both a tool and a test of your reverence for Christ.
- At Love and Respect conferences, I dramatize Sarah pointing her finger at me, frustrated, while Jesus stands behind her saying, "Unto me, Emerson. Do this unto me."
- Sarah has her own version when I stonewall: "Yes, Sarah, I know he wrote the *Love & Respect* book, but unto Me, Sarah. Unto Me."
- You must be reminded that your real audience is Christ. Thus, "as to the Lord."
- This isn't about ignoring problems but responding with Christ in view.

Key Scriptures:

- Ephesians 6:7: Serve as to the Lord.
- Ephesians 5:21: Submit out of reverence for Christ.
- Matthew 25:40: What you do for others, you do for Christ.

Key Takeaways:

- Marriage is a tool and a test to deepen and demonstrate our love and reverence for Christ.
- Your spouse can't stop you from loving and reverencing Christ.
- Even if your love or respect goes unnoticed, God sees.
- You don't love and respect your spouse for their reaction but because you love and reverence Jesus beyond their shoulder.
- Every act of love or respect touches the heart of Christ.

Notes

Use this space to jot down what moved you, challenged you, or gave you fresh perspective.

Group Discussion [30 TO 45 MINUTES]

Enjoy this time of connection. Remember, what you share in the group may be just what someone else needed to hear.

Pick a question from below that resonates with you. This is a space for personal insight and encouragement, not for fixing your spouse or confessing their faults. That's not appropriate here.

Some couples will share more, others may listen. That's okay. Listening can bring clarity; sharing brings hope, especially for those quietly struggling.

If you tend to talk easily, leave space for others. And if you're usually quiet, consider speaking up.

Make sure everyone who wants to share has a chance. Just because someone is quiet doesn't mean they aren't eager to contribute. They may simply be waiting for the right moment.

Group Reflection Prompts

(You do not have enough time to answer all, so choose your adventure!)

1. What story that I told in the teaching spoke to your heart?
2. What truth from Scripture stood out to you?
3. How does remembering how God sees us as blameless and uncondemned, and as co-heirs with Christ, ease pressure in daily life?
4. Did "doing marriage unto the Lord" switch on a light for you?
5. What would it mean to pause and picture Jesus saying, "I see that. That matters to Me"?
6. Was there a testimony from a couple in the video that really connected with you? (Like the husband remembering Jesus stands beyond his wife's shoulder, so he said to his wife humorously during conflict, "Go ahead . . . make my day. Let me show Jesus my love as you disrespect me.")
7. How might viewing your marriage as a tool and test to love and reverence Jesus reshape your interactions?
8. What does it mean that "your spouse can't stop you from doing marriage unto the Lord"?
9. What changes when we stop trying to earn worth from each other and rest in God's?
10. What does it mean to see your love or respect as an act of worship that Jesus notices?

Husband and Wife Discussion [5 TO 15 MINUTES]

Take a few minutes as a couple to talk privately, however that works best in your setting.

This isn't about fixing each other. It's a chance to pause, reflect, and reconnect, not just with one another, but with the Lord. Keep it positive, personal, and pointed toward the Lord speaking to you.

There's no pressure or perfect answer. Just a brief, meaningful exchange between the two of you. Choose one or two questions below that feel most positive to you. You cannot cover them all, but read them all to yourself and select the ones that guide you to communicate what inspires and uplifts you.

Remember: You'll have a fifteen-minute check-in later this week. This conversation can simply set the stage for that.

Conversation Starters

1. Was there a truth tonight about who you are in Christ that encouraged you?
2. What stood out to you about the idea that your value is God-given?
3. How do you feel personally about this statement: "I am who God says I am"?
4. How might it change things this week to picture Jesus standing beyond your shoulders?
5. What's one small thing you could do this week that quietly says, "Lord, this is for You"?
6. Which truth from Scripture would you like to carry into this week (e.g., blameless, bought with a price, no condemnation, priceless, child of God)?
7. What does it mean to you that Jesus notices your efforts in your marriage, even the quiet ones?
8. Do you believe this: "Your spouse can't stop you from doing marriage unto the Lord"?
9. How does this impact you: "Jesus sees everything—not to shame you, but to say, 'Atta boy. Atta girl.'"
10. In the group discussion, did someone share something that encouraged you?

Group Prayer [5 TO 10 MINUTES]

Come back together as a group. Close by thanking God for the chance to draw closer to Him and to one another.

Thank Him for the truth of His Word and that your worth is anchored in Christ, not in your performance or your spouse's opinion.

Ask the Lord to help you see Jesus standing just beyond your spouse's shoulder; someone He deeply loves and will one day glorify throughout eternity.

No matter what you're feeling in the moment, invite God to help you respond in love and respect, not because your spouse always deserves it, but because *He* is always worthy.

Ask for the grace to live your marriage "unto Him," taking every opportunity to show your devotion to Christ through how you love and respect each other.

SESSION ONE

PERSONAL STUDY

This is your time to reflect on the truths you explored about identity and intent. You'll go through it individually, as will your spouse.

Start with the **Biblical Foundation** and then move to **Practical Application**. I've included plenty for you to consider, not to overwhelm you but to offer options. Skim through the material, and then focus where the Lord seems to nudge you. Don't try to act on everything. Just ask, "Lord, what one or two truths should I lean into this week?"

Remember: We all tend to gravitate toward our *felt* needs, but that doesn't always mean we're focused on our *true* needs. For example, if I challenge a husband to reflect on the ways his wife may be showing him disrespect, he'll likely zero in on that because it feels urgent and personal. That's his felt need. But if I challenge him instead to consider how he might better love his wife, that could actually be the deeper *true* need. And if he's anything like me, he'll still find himself focusing more on the respect issue! That's the human struggle all of us have, including wives. Felt needs shout! True needs whisper.

Also, plan a fifteen-minute **Weekly Check-In** with your spouse later this week. You'll see that section after the personal study material. This isn't meant to be a deep heart-to-heart but a brief, encouraging touchpoint. You can even do it by phone if needed. As you study, jot down what specifically encouraged you so you'll have something to share. Make it personal, positive, and point it toward what God is doing in you.

If you're reading *Lightbulb Moments in Marriage* alongside this, review the **Introduction** and **chapters 1–2** this week. When you check in with your spouse, feel free to share anything for that reading, but be sure to include **what encouraged you most.**

I want to be clear about one thing: Don't use this as a way to indirectly critique your spouse. For example, "I was encouraged to learn that you're the main issue in our marriage because of your poor self-worth and co-dependency. You expect me to be God and heal you. Even so, it helped me feel better about myself and how to navigate the marriage with you."

That's not encouragement. That's blame dressed up as reflection. Keep the focus on your heart and God's work in you, not what you think your spouse needs to change.

Also, if one of you is quiet or unsure of what to say, that's okay. Some process inwardly. Give each other grace and space. Be patient. One spouse may want this to spark deeper connection or instant healing, and while that's understandable, this isn't the time for pressure.

The goal is simple: Share what encouraged you.

Let that be enough. Deeper connection may come later, but for now, aim for shared encouragement, not problem-solving.

LIGHTBULB MOMENT #1:

GOD-GIVEN, NOT SPOUSE-DRIVEN

Biblical Foundation

Your identity is not something you earn through your spouse's approval. It is established by God, revealed in Scripture, and grounded in Christ. The verses below were written to early believers navigating hardship, identity confusion, and persecution. For us today, they still speak with power and clarity. These truths are not just emotional comfort. They are revelations from the heart of God.

1 Corinthians 1:8

"[Jesus Christ] will also confirm you to the end, blameless on the day of our Lord Jesus Christ" (NASB).

Paul wrote this to the Corinthian church, a group of believers who were struggling with immaturity, division, and pride. Yet Paul opens his letter with this astonishing truth: In Christ, they were already considered **blameless** before God.

Blameless here refers to legal acquittal in the divine courtroom, based not on their behavior but on the righteousness of Christ applied to them by faith. Despite their flaws, they were declared righteous.

Corinth was a city marked by status-seeking, public shame, and performance. This statement turned their culture upside-down: God had already rendered the final verdict.

1 Corinthians 6:20

"You were bought with a price" (ESV).

This is a reference to the Roman slave market, a metaphor the early church would have understood well. Paul reminds believers that their freedom came at a **cost**: the death of Christ. The word *bought* implies a change in ownership and a permanent new status. You are no longer your own. You now belong to Christ—not to public opinion, not to your past, and certainly not to your spouse's evaluation.

To be "bought" with a price in Roman culture meant permanent freedom from previous masters. Paul uses that cultural reality to remind Christians that they are now free from condemnation and shame.

Romans 8:1

"There is now no condemnation for those who are in Christ Jesus."

Paul, writing to a mixed group of Jewish and Gentile believers, makes a definitive legal declaration: The gavel has come down and the verdict is "no condemnation." This is judicial language from a Roman court. The believer in Christ is not just forgiven; they are legally and eternally declared "not guilty." This removes any spiritual performance pressure from the relationship between God and the believer.

In Roman law, condemnation carried public shame and loss of rights. Paul says those in Christ have been publicly released from that shame . . . forever.

Romans 8:17

"If children, heirs also, heirs of God and fellow heirs with Christ" (NASB).

This was a radical idea in both Jewish and Roman worlds: Men and women alike, slave and free, Jew and Gentile, were given the same spiritual inheritance as Christ.

Being a "co-heir" doesn't just mean inclusion; it means equal standing. Everything the Father gave the Son is also promised to those who are adopted into His family.

Under Roman adoption law, a child adopted into a family had the same rights as a biological child, including inheritance. Paul uses this legal reality to assure believers of their secured, eternal inheritance with Christ.

1 John 3:1

"See how great a love the Father has given us, that we should be called children of God; and in fact we are" (NASB).

John is writing to reassure a persecuted church that their identity is anchored in God's love, not in their circumstances or status in the world.

"Children of God" is not a symbolic title; it is a new reality. The verb *given* (Greek *dedōken*) indicates an act completed in the past with ongoing results. You **are** His child and always will be.

The early believers were often rejected by family and society. John counters this rejection with a greater truth: They were part of God's eternal family. No earthly relationship could revoke that status.

Summary

Your identity is not fragile. It is anchored in God's redemptive work through Christ. In a culture that bases worth on performance, reputation, or affirmation, Scripture declares:

- You are **blameless** in Christ (1 Corinthians 1:8).
- You were **bought** at a high price (1 Corinthians 6:20).
- You are **not condemned** (Romans 8:1).
- You are a **co-heir** with Christ (Romans 8:17).
- You are a **beloved child** of God (1 John 3:1).

These truths were written to people in real turmoil. And they still stand today—unchanging, immovable, and unshaken by anything in your marriage.

Reflection

- ◆ Which of these five truths (blameless, bought, not condemned, co-heir, beloved child) speaks most directly to your heart today? Why?

- ◆ Do you find it easier to believe these truths about others than about yourself? Why might that be?

- ◆ Which identity-truth challenges your current way of thinking the most? What do you think the Holy Spirit is trying to reveal through that tension?

- ◆ Which historical insight (slave market, Roman courtroom, adoption laws) helped you better grasp your secure standing in Christ?

- ◆ What false label (e.g., failure, unlovable, not enough) do you need to lay down in exchange for your true identity in Christ?

- ◆ How could anchoring your self-worth in God's verdict transform the way you listen, speak, and love this week?

LIGHTBULB MOMENT #1:

GOD-GIVEN, NOT SPOUSE-DRIVEN

Practical Application

The truths you just studied were written to real people in real turmoil. They didn't have perfect marriages, emotional security, or societal affirmation. And yet Scripture declared their identity fixed in Christ: blameless, bought, not condemned, co-heirs, beloved children.

So now what? How do we live out these truths, especially in marriage, where it can be easy to let our spouse's reaction shape our self-perception?

This section is designed to help you take the theological truth and make it relationally personal. Let God speak to your heart about where you still look to a spouse for what only He can provide and how rooting your worth in Him might reshape the way you live, love, respect, and grow.

Emotional Well-Being in Marriage

- On a scale of 1 to 10, how much does your emotional well-being in marriage tend to rise or fall based on your spouse's mood, tone, or reaction?

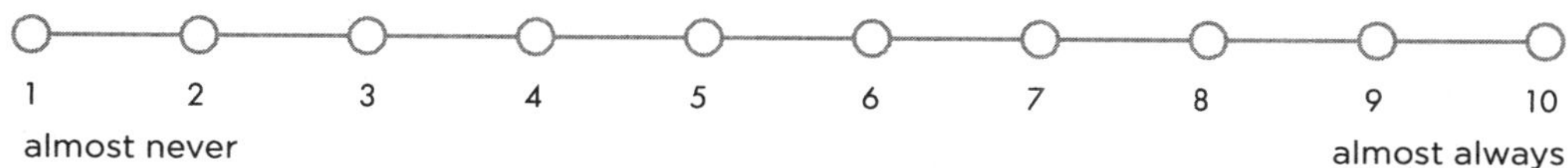

- If your number was 6 or higher, think of a recent moment when your spouse's demeanor felt like it defined your worth. What did you feel internally? How might Christ's verdict have changed how you saw yourself in that moment?

Shaping Versus Defining

"Sarah doesn't define me, but she does refine me."

This line emphasizes the difference between letting your spouse shape you versus define you. It's possible to stay teachable without losing emotional stability.

- How do you usually respond when your spouse gives honest feedback or brings up a concern?

  - ❑ I shut down or get defensive.
  - ❑ I try, but it's hard not to take it personally.
  - ❑ I can receive it calmly and grow from it.

- What kind of feedback is hardest for you to hear from your spouse? Why do you think that hits you so deeply?

Identity Truth

- Choose one identity truth that stood out most clearly from Scripture:

  - ❑ I am blameless in Christ.
  - ❑ I was bought with a price.
  - ❑ I am not condemned.
  - ❑ I am a co-heir with Christ.
  - ❑ I am a beloved child of God.

- In what ways do you need this truth to anchor you when your spouse is distant, critical, withdrawn, or silent?

- What difference could it make if you held on to this identity instead of the moment?

- How does God's view of you anchor you when you're feeling discouraged in the marriage?

- What practical steps can you take to shift your identity from spouse-driven to God-given?

Spiritual Security

- What might change in your marriage if you felt secure enough in Christ to receive correction without slipping into self-doubt? Consider how spiritual security might reshape your everyday interactions:

- How would you listen differently during hard conversations?
- How might it influence your tone, body language, or emotional posture?
- What would trusting God's verdict free you from in those moments?

Practical Reminder

♦ What's one practical way you'll remind yourself this week that your value is God-given? Examples:

- A verse on the mirror
- A lock-screen Scripture
- A short breath-prayer like "I am who You say I am"
- A journal entry each morning
- Writing your identity truths and posting them where you'll see them

♦ What specific plan will help you rehearse God's truth until it replaces old narratives?

Possible Check-In Statements

When it's time for your fifteen-minute Check-In with your spouse, here are a few simple and encouraging ways to share what helped you:

- "This week I was reminded that I'm blameless in Christ, and that helped me stay more grounded."
- "The image of being 'bought at a price' helped me see my incredible worth to God."
- "Realizing there's no condemnation gave me courage to try again after I messed up—and without spiraling into shame."

You don't have to live on borrowed approval anymore. You're not defined by how well you're liked, affirmed, or understood today. You are not on trial. The verdict is in, and it's eternal.

LIGHTBULB MOMENT #2

SEEING JESUS BEYOND THE SHOULDER OF OUR SPOUSE

Biblical Foundation

This Lightbulb Moment invites a powerful shift in perspective: What if your marriage is ultimately not just about you and your spouse but about you and Christ?

When you begin to see Jesus standing just beyond the shoulder of your spouse, everything changes. Your tone, your patience, and your words become opportunities to show your love and reverence for Him.

As I often say, "Your spouse affords you the opportunity to touch the very heart of Christ."

Colossians 3:23–24

"Whatever you do, do your work heartily, as for the Lord and not for people, knowing that it is from the Lord that you will receive the reward of the inheritance. It is the Lord Christ whom you serve" (NASB).

That phrase "whatever you do" includes your marriage. It includes how you treat your spouse in moments of joy and in moments of frustration. Whether or not your spouse responds well, you can still choose to love or respect them *unto the Lord.*

In fact, the immediate context of this verse refers to slaves serving their masters. If God called slaves—who had no freedom, status, or fair treatment—to serve with sincerity as unto Christ, then surely husbands and wives, who have chosen each other in covenant love, are without excuse (Ephesians 5:21–22, 25).

If we lack a vision for living this out in marriage, we're missing something sacred and essential.

Reflection

- How does this reframe your motivation in a moment when your spouse is unresponsive or unkind?

Ephesians 5:21–22, 25

"Submit to one another out of reverence for Christ. Wives, submit yourselves to your own husbands as you do to the Lord. . . . Husbands, love your wives, just as Christ loved the church and gave himself up for her."

These aren't just relational instructions; they're acts of worship.

I've learned that marriage becomes both a tool and a test to express my love and reverence for Christ. Even when Sarah doesn't respond how I'd hoped, I can still respond in love . . . unto Jesus.

Reflection

♦ Which phrase most challenges or inspires you right now?

- "Out of reverence for Christ"?
- "As to the Lord"?
- "Just as Christ loved"?

Matthew 25:40

"As you've done it to the least of these, you've done it unto Me" (paraphrased).

That includes your spouse. When you love your spouse, even when it's not returned, you're loving Christ. When you respect your spouse, even when you feel overlooked, you're reverencing Christ.

This isn't about pretending the pain isn't real. It's about remembering: Your response still matters to Jesus.

Reflection

♦ How might remembering that Jesus sees your love and respect change the way you respond in conflict?

Ephesians 6:7–8

"Serve wholeheartedly, as if you were serving the Lord, not people, because you know that the Lord will reward each one for whatever good they do."

Even when your spouse doesn't notice your efforts, God sees. And He promises to reward every act of love and respect offered unto Him. Your unseen faithfulness is never forgotten.

Reflection

♦ What comfort does this give you when your spouse seems to overlook your efforts?

♦ Take a quiet moment now to picture Jesus standing just behind your spouse's shoulder. He's not watching to criticize. He's whispering: "I see that. It matters to Me." How does that image change the way you want to show up at home or outside the home this week?

Possible Check-In Statements

If you need help wording something from this section during your Check-In, here are a couple of examples:

- "This week I was reminded from the Scriptures that my words and actions in marriage are part of how I worship Christ, and that really helped reframe my daily mindset. I know I fall short, but it encouraged me to remember that Jesus simply wants me to keep seeing Him."

- "It encouraged me to think about serving the Lord wholeheartedly as the apostle Paul revealed, not to prove anything, but to honor the Lord in how I show up. He is present. What surprised me was how quickly I can take my eyes off Him, and how gently He keeps drawing me back."

LIGHTBULB MOMENT #2

SEEING JESUS BEYOND THE SHOULDER OF OUR SPOUSE

Practical Application

Now that we've explored what the Bible says about living unto Christ, I want to help you take a few moments to apply those truths in ways you may not have considered before.

This is not just about trying harder; it's about seeing differently. When we reframe, we have a lightbulb moment. In fact, researchers call this "cognitive restructuring," a process where we replace distorted thinking with clearer, more constructive truth. It's also linked to what psychologists call transformational learning or a paradigm shift, when a moment of tension or crisis becomes the catalyst for a new, deeper understanding.

We have a lightbulb moment when we reframe. And when we reframe through the lens of Christ, it becomes not just psychological insight but spiritual renewal.

As I've said, marriage is both a tool and a test. Both are about seeing Jesus beyond the shoulder of your spouse.

A **tool** is something God uses to form and sharpen your love and reverence for Christ. In marriage, that formation happens through the daily call to trust and obey Him, especially in the small, unseen, or difficult moments.

A **test** reveals how deeply you love and revere Jesus, not to shame you for falling short, but to affirm your growth. It's not a test designed to make you feel small. It's a test your Father uses to say, "I see you. You're learning to walk with Me." It's a positive test, one that reveals you're getting it. And in those moments, I believe He whispers to your heart: **"Atta boy." "Atta girl."**

A Tool and a Test

- On a scale of 1 to 10, with 1 being "not at all" and 10 being "all the time," to what degree do you view your marriage as both a tool and a test to deepen your love and reverence for Christ?

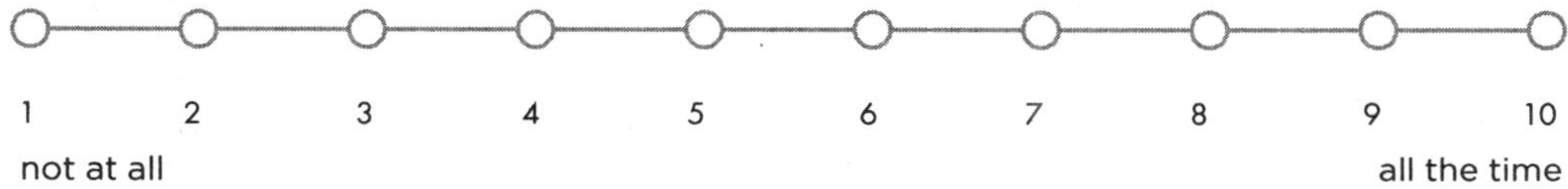

- ♦ If your number was a **6 or higher**: Recall a recent moment when you responded in a loving or respectful way, even when your spouse didn't respond in kind. What helped you remember you were doing it unto Christ? How did that affect the tone in your home?

- ♦ If your number was a **5 or lower**: What makes it most difficult for you to keep Jesus in view, standing just beyond your spouse's shoulder, inviting you to love and reverence Him in that moment?

When the Pressure Builds

When tension rises, it's easy to lose sight of the sacred and focus only on the situation. That's the moment we shift from unto Him to onto them.

Below are common responses from couples who forget that Jesus is present and watching. Again, this is not to shame but to affirm what we're all working through.

- ♦ Which of these do you recognize in yourself? After each one, reflect on how it might be impacting your marriage.
    - Pulling back or withdrawing when criticized
    - Justifying yourself instead of listening
    - Letting your spouse's bad day define your mood
    - Feeling invisible or "not enough" and shutting down
    - Reacting defensively instead of staying teachable

- ♦ What might change if, in one of these moments—moments that can feel unfair—you paused, looked "beyond the shoulder," and heard the Lord whisper, "Unto Me . . . that's it . . . you're loving and reverencing Me"?

A Sacred Pause

Take two minutes. Close your eyes and picture Jesus standing just beyond your spouse's shoulder. He's not angry. He's attentive. He sees your effort, your restraint, your longing to do what's right. He's whispering encouragement, not condemnation.

The Bible calls us to fix our eyes on Jesus, the author and perfecter of our faith (Hebrews 12:2).

It says the eyes of our heart can be enlightened to know the hope and power we have in Him (Ephesians 1:18–20).

And even when we don't see Him, we can still love Him, believe in Him, and be filled with joy: "Though you have not seen him, you love him; and even though you do not see him now, you believe in him and are filled with an inexpressible and glorious joy" (1 Peter 1:8). Let this moment be about seeing Jesus with the eyes of faith, not just seeing your spouse.

- ♦ What might He be saying to you right now?
- ♦ What "something greater" could He be calling you to, something that reflects deeper love and reverence for Christ?

When God Sees What Others Don't

Paul wrote, "The Lord will reward each one for whatever good they do" (Ephesians 6:8). That means every choice to love or respect, even when it goes unnoticed, is seen by God and treasured by Christ.

Nothing done unto Him is ever wasted.

- ♦ How does it encourage you to know that your efforts to love and respect your spouse are acts of love and reverence for Christ?
- ♦ What is one small, practical way you can remind yourself this week, perhaps through a note, prayer, or pause, to do what you do unto the Lord?

Closing Thought

When I picture Jesus standing just beyond Sarah's shoulder, everything shifts. I'm no longer reacting to a spouse, I'm responding to the Savior. And when I choose love and respect unto Him, I can almost hear His gentle approval: "Atta boy. Atta girl. Unto Me."

I must remember: Every touch, every word I speak . . . moves the heart of the Christ I seek.

Possible Check-In Statements

Here are two ways someone might word what they're learning in this area during the fifteen-minute Check-In time:

- "It helped me this week to think about how small acts in marriage can still be part of loving and reverencing Jesus. That was a new thought for me, and it gave me peace."
- "The idea of marriage being a tool and a test really stayed with me, not in a heavy way, but in a hopeful way. It reminded me that Jesus is with me as I keep learning."

Weekly Check-In

A Shared Reflection

This week, after working through the personal study, take fifteen minutes together to share your key takeaways.

Keep it simple, grace-filled, and focused on what encouraged you. This isn't therapy or a place to critique each other. Instead, reflect on how God is at work in your own heart.

Perfection isn't the goal. Progress is. What matters most is that you both show up with humility, curiosity, and a desire to grow.

Remember: One of you may share more than the other, and that's okay. Don't try to match emotions. Just meet each other where you are, with kindness.

Resist thinking, *I hope you're applying this.* Instead ask, "Lord, what are You showing me—regardless of how fair it feels?" This posture protects connection and invites change in the right spirit.

Encouragement for Wives and Husbands

Wives—If your husband seems quiet or reserved, don't assume he's uninterested. He may be unsure how to engage or hesitant from past experiences. Many men feel they're "the problem" in marriage discussions, and that can create inner resistance. Your support and belief in his goodwill can create the safety he needs to engage.

Husbands—If your wife is enthusiastic, don't interpret that as criticism. Her desire is often for deeper closeness, not correction. Small gestures of engagement from you—like a question or a short comment—can mean more than you realize.

This study isn't about fixing each other. It's about letting Christ shape both of you through humility and grace.

Suggested Questions [PICK 2 TO 3]

Lightbulb #1—God-Given, Not Spouse-Driven

- What helped you see your worth more clearly through God's eyes?
- Did you notice moments you sought affirmation from your spouse or others?
- How did this truth help you stay grounded in Christ?

Lightbulb #2—Seeing Jesus Beyond the Shoulder of Our Spouse

- How did "unto Me" reshape your view of how you respond in marriage?
- Was there a moment when you sensed Christ watching your interaction?
- What gives you strength to love or respect even when it's not returned?

When Tension Rises

- If the Crazy Cycle (without love she reacts without respect and without respect he reacts without love) began spinning, how did you respond?
- What could it look like to stay anchored in Christ in those moments?

Looking Ahead

Read **chapters 3–4** in *Lightbulb Moments in Marriage* before the next group. Highlight anything that encouraged you, challenged your assumptions, or gave language to something you've felt but couldn't express. Use the space below to note what you might want to share next week.

BEFORE GROUP MEETING	Read chapters 3–4 in *Lightbulb Moments in Marriage* Read the Welcome section (page 26)
GROUP MEETING	Discuss the Connect questions (pages 26–27) Watch the video teaching for session 2 and take notes (pages 27–30) Engage in a Group Discussion on the material (pages 30–31) Couples have a Husband and Wife Discussion (pages 31–32) Close in Group Prayer (page 32)
PERSONAL STUDY	
LIGHTBULB MOMENT #3: BIBLICAL FOUNDATION	Complete the Biblical Foundation personal study for Lightbulb Moment #3 (pages 34–36)
LIGHTBULB MOMENT #3: PRACTICAL APPLICATION	Complete the Practical Application personal study for Lightbulb Moment #3 (pages 37–38)
LIGHTBULB MOMENT #4: BIBLICAL FOUNDATION	Complete the Biblical Foundation personal study for Lightbulb Moment #4 (pages 39–41)
LIGHTBULB MOMENT #4: PRACTICAL APPLICATION	Complete the Practical Application personal study for Lightbulb Moment #4 (pages 42–45)
WEEKLY CHECK-IN	Connect with your spouse during the week to discuss your key insights from this session (pages 46–47)
BEFORE NEXT WEEK	Read chapters 5–6 in *Lightbulb Moments in Marriage*

SESSION TWO

OUR ETERNITY AND OUR WORLDVIEW

LIGHTBULB #3:

Living with "Well Done!" in Mind

Your marriage carries eternal significance in God's story—every act of love and respect matters to Him and will not go unrewarded.

LIGHTBULB #4:

The Holy Word, Not Hollywood

Hollywood's reel love feels real because it promises excitement and ease. But only the Holy Word reveals joy, wisdom, and our eternal purpose God designed for marriage.

Welcome [READ ON YOUR OWN]

Scripture reminds us, "To be absent from the body [is] to be at home with the Lord" (2 Corinthians 5:8 NASB).

That moment is coming. One day, we will be in the presence of Jesus Christ, and Scripture says He will reward His forgiven followers for the good they've done in this life.

Lightbulb Moment #3 points us to that future moment when we stand before the Lord and hear the words, "Well done, good and faithful servant!" (Matthew 25:21).

Your marriage plays a vital part in that story. Every time you obey God's commands—loving or respecting your spouse in faithfulness to the forgiving Christ—it touches His heart. And it will not go unnoticed or unrewarded.

This eternal perspective changes how we see everything—including our daily decisions in marriage. It reminds us that even if our spouse doesn't respond the way we hope, we can still do marriage God's way. And we can live with joy now, knowing our obedience pleases Christ.

Lightbulb Moment #4 builds on this by asking: *Whose voice are you listening to in your marriage—the world's or God's? Are you living by the Holy Word or by Hollywood?*

Culture is constantly whispering its version of "reel" love—telling us what we deserve, what we're missing, or what we should demand. But Scripture points to a different path: a sacred covenant designed by God to reflect His love, glory, and truth.

I had to settle this personally early in my walk with Christ. Raised in a non-Christian home, I came to believe in the authority of Scripture. And it changed everything—including how I saw marriage.

Jesus said, "Man shall not live on bread alone, but on every word that comes out of the mouth of God" (Matthew 4:4 NASB).

That's my foundation. And it can be yours too, if it is not already.

So today, you are invited to reflect on these two lightbulb moments:

- Your eternity matters—and your marriage plays a role in it.
- Your worldview matters—and Scripture must shape how you live.

Connect [5 TO 15 MINUTES]

If you or any of the couples in your group don't know each other yet, take a moment to introduce yourselves. Then use the prompts below to ease into today's session.

Prompt 1—Our Eternity: Living with "Well Done!" in Mind

When you hear the word *eternity*, what comes to mind? Do you ever think about standing before Jesus one day and hearing the words, *"Well done, good and faithful servant"* (Matthew 25:21)? How often do you think about that moment? What pushes that perspective to the background in daily life—and how might it change the way you live if you kept it more in view?

Take a moment to reflect and share. There's no formula here—just honest thoughts about what eternity means and how it might shape everyday decisions, including marriage.

Prompt 2—Our Worldview: The Holy Word, Not Hollywood

Culture constantly speaks—through social media, entertainment, and even well-meaning advice. Its messages emphasize personal happiness, instant connection, or surface-level romance. In contrast, God's Word calls us to something deeper—love that serves, respects, and endures.

What are some truths from Scripture that have helped you see marriage in a richer, more meaningful way? How have biblical principles—like grace, humility, forgiveness, or faithfulness—shaped the way you think about your role as a spouse?

As you reflect, share ways you've been encouraged or challenged by God's truth. What have you come to value more deeply in your marriage as you've sought to align your heart with His design?

Reflection Thought

As you talk, notice how these topics—eternity and worldview—connect to this week's theme. Eternity reminds us who we ultimately live for. God's Word reminds us how we're called to live.

The world often says to follow your feelings or focus on what makes you happiest in the moment. But Scripture points to something far richer: a way of life that honors God and leads to deeper joy, trust, and connection in the long run.

This isn't about ignoring romance or settling for less. It's about building something more—something grounded, lasting, and life-giving. When a couple follows God's design, they tend to experience the kind of relationship the world promises but rarely delivers.

And that kind of faithfulness? It matters to Christ. It echoes in eternity.

It's the kind of life that hears, *"Well done."*

Watch [30 TO 40 MINUTES]

As you watch, jot down any thoughts that speak to your heart. Many key ideas are already outlined here so you can stay fully present.

Outline: Lightbulb Moments #3 & #4

I. Lightbulb Moment #3—Our Eternity: Living with "Well Done!" in Mind

- The "Well Done" Moment
  - One day, you'll stand before Jesus. He will say, *"Well done, good and faithful servant."*
  - Marriage is temporary. But how we live in it matters forever.

- A Glimpse of Eternal Joy
  - Think of the joy of receiving a long-hoped-for gift. That moment—*"aaaah!"*—is just a shadow of the joy we'll feel when we enter Christ's presence. I call it *the endless first moment*.
- My Mother's Eternal Lens
  - Before she died in 2001, my mom wrote a poem about heaven. She lived with eternity in view, and that still undoes me.
- Obedience, Even If Your Spouse Doesn't Respond
  - You can do marriage God's way, even if your spouse doesn't.
  - Jesus sees every act of faithfulness, even when it isn't noticed by others.
- Eternal Rewards
  - Salvation is a gift. But reward is about faithfulness.
  - If Jesus intends to reward you, let Him.

Key Scriptures:

- Ephesians 6:8: The Lord rewards each one for whatever good they do.
- 1 Corinthians 3:14: The builder will receive a reward if their work survives.
- Colossians 3:24: You'll receive an inheritance from the Lord.
- Romans 8:17: We are co-heirs with Christ.

Two Testimonies:

- *A husband*: "I used to chase affirmation. Now I ask, 'Is He pleased?'"
- *A wife*: "I stopped clinging to fairness—and started clinging to faithfulness."

- Imagine That Day
  - Many who feel like they're failing may hear, *"Well done."*
  - Every act of love and respect matters to Christ—and He will reward it.

II. Lightbulb Moment #4—Our Worldview: The Holy Word, Not Hollywood

- Reel Love vs. Real Love
  - A friend nearly ended her relationship after watching *Funny Girl*.
  - Someone asked, "Are you into REEL love—or REAL love?" That changed everything.
- Misleading Expectations
  - One man said, "I nearly walked away—not because my wife didn't love me, but because she didn't act like women in movies."
  - He realized his wife was designed to respond to real love—not fantasy.

- My Own Turning Point
    - Early in my journey, I had to decide: Would I live by Scripture or culture?
    - Jesus kept saying, *"It is written."* That settled it for me.

Key Scriptures:

- Matthew 4:4: Man lives by every word from God.
- Hebrews 1:1–2: God has spoken to us through His Son.
- 2 Timothy 3:16–17: All Scripture is God-breathed and equips us.

- What the Bible Says About Marriage
    - Marriage is a covenant. It reflects God's image and Christ's love for the church.
    - Faithfulness in marriage honors God—even when no one else sees.
- Real Love Obeys
    - Jesus said, "The wise man hears My words and acts on them."
    - Hollywood says, "Follow your heart." Jesus says, "Follow Me."
- The Final Question
    - Which voice shapes your marriage: **Hollywood or the Holy Word?**

Notes

Write down what most encouraged or challenged you.

Notes

Group Discussion [30 TO 45 MINUTES]

Group guidelines reminder when focusing on Lightbulb Moments #3 and #4:

- Freely select the question that prompts a response from you. You won't be able to answer all, so choose your adventure!
- We talk about what God is showing us, not what our spouse should be doing.

Group Reflection Prompts

1. I shared a story about a kid receiving a bicycle on Christmas morning and his breathless "*aaaah!*" moment of joy. Have you ever experienced a moment like that? Why might that help you picture what it will feel like to hear Jesus say, "*Well done*"?
2. I also told you about my mother's final poem, written with eternity in view. What would it look like to carry that kind of eternal mindset into your marriage—even in small ways? Is there someone in your life whose eternal perspective has shaped the way you think about marriage or life?

3. I reminded you that your faithfulness matters to Christ, even when things aren't easy or ideal. Why might that truth bring hope to people in all kinds of marriages . . . good, hard, or somewhere in between?
4. Marriage is temporary. But how we do marriage matters, because how we love and respect one another is, in the end, about how we love and reverence Christ. How does it help you to know that Jesus sees the little things, even when no one else notices?
5. Let's go deeper. What excites or inspires you most about the thought of hearing *"well done"* from Jesus Himself? How does it change things to realize your marriage actually plays a role in that eternal moment?
6. Can you picture yourself walking into His presence and hearing those words? What do you think you'll feel? Joy, relief, maybe tears?
7. I asked, "Are you living by Hollywood or the Holy Word?" What are some ways our culture gives us distorted or unrealistic expectations about marriage? What helps you catch those messages before they start shaping your thinking?
8. I shared how movies and media can distort how we think about love, intimacy, and connection. What's one message, in your opinion, that people commonly believe about marriage that doesn't line up with Scripture? Why is it so easy to believe those ideas, even when we know they're off?
9. I also said, "If Scripture clearly says it, I'm standing with Scripture." Why is that kind of decision essential today, especially in how we view marriage?
10. We all face moments where we can either follow our feelings or follow God's Word. What helps you stay grounded when life or marriage feels overwhelming? Is there a verse or truth that's helped anchor you in those moments?

Husband and Wife Discussion [5 TO 15 MINUTES]

A Note Before You Begin

Keep this conversation focused on **yourself**, not your spouse. Try statements like:

- "God is showing me . . . "
- "I want to grow in . . . "

Even good intentions can miss the mark if they:

- Make the other feel small or defensive
- Include sarcasm or spiritual correction

These questions are designed to inspire reflection, not assign blame.

Conversation Starters

1. What part of the "well done" message stuck with you? Why?
2. How does it change things to know Jesus sees every act of faithfulness?
3. What's one small choice or habit that might matter for eternity, even if no one else notices?
4. Have you ever viewed your marriage as a ministry that matters to Christ?
5. What's one "everyday" part of marriage that might matter more to God than we realize?
6. What could help you stay mindful of eternal reward in everyday marriage moments?
7. What's one marriage expectation you now realize came from culture, not God? (Don't say, "I realize I must learn to live with a sinful, fallen person, so have to let go of reasonable expectations for a happy marriage.")
8. What would you say to someone who compares their marriage to movies or social media?
9. Is there a verse or truth that's anchored you when the marriage felt hard due to normal challenges? (Remember, when you listen, refrain from saying, "What are you saying—that I cause your challenges?" Instead reply with, "That's meaningful how the Lord is revealing to you how to be anchored in His truth. Thank you for sharing." Most of us don't make these unwise comments—but some do!)
10. What helps you base decisions on Scripture instead of feelings or trends?

Group Prayer [5 TO 10 MINUTES]

End your time by thanking Jesus for His sacrifice and the eternal hope He's given you and for the chance to reflect on what truly matters in marriage.

You can invite someone to pray aloud or keep the time quiet and personal. Either way, let the focus be:

- Gratitude for Christ's love and forgiveness
- Humility as we grow in faithfulness
- Clarity to see our marriage through an eternal lens
- Strength to live by the Word, not the world
- Hope that even the smallest steps of faithfulness are seen and will be rewarded

You could pray: *"Jesus, thank You that You see us, know us, and love us. Thank You for reminding us that nothing we do in faith is ever wasted. Help us live with eternity in mind. Let Your Word, and not the world, shape our marriage."*

SESSION TWO

PERSONAL STUDY

The Lightbulb Moment that how you treat your spouse (and others) has eternal significance can be a momentous insight. It can also be eye-opening to realize just how much of Hollywood's *reel* love has influenced your perspective on *real* love! In this week's personal study, you will mine the riches of God's Holy Word to gain further insights into these principles and how to apply them to your marriage. Continue to write down some of your responses to the questions so you will have a couple notes for when you meet with your spouse. If you are reading *Lightbulb Moments in Marriage* alongside this study, first read chapters 3–4 of the book.

LIGHTBULB MOMENT #3

LIVING WITH "WELL DONE!" IN MIND

Biblical Foundation

Matthew 25:21

"Well done, good and faithful servant! You have been faithful with a few things; I will put you in charge of many things. Come and share your master's happiness!"

Jesus spoke these words in the context of the Parable of the Talents, delivered during His final week before the crucifixion. The setting is weighty. Israel lived under Roman occupation, and Jesus was preparing His followers for life without His physical presence. The parable addresses how believers are to live *between* His departure and His return.

In the story, the master entrusts resources to his servants and then leaves. When he returns, he evaluates not their success compared to one another but their faithfulness with what they were given. The servant is praised not for greatness but for stewardship.

For first-century believers, this teaching clarified that obedience mattered even when Christ seemed absent and circumstances felt uncertain. Faithfulness was not optional; it was expected.

For believers throughout history, this passage establishes a lasting truth: God's final evaluation is not based on visibility, talent, or outcomes but on faithfulness. The promise of "entering the joy of your master" points to a future participation in Christ's reign and joy—something far greater than earthly reward.

Ephesians 6:7–8

"Serve wholeheartedly, as if you were serving the Lord, not people, because you know that the Lord will reward each one for whatever good they do."

Paul wrote these words to believers living within a rigid Roman social structure. The immediate audience included slaves and free persons alike—people with vastly different levels of power, autonomy, and recognition. In that culture, slaves were often invisible, undervalued, and easily abused.

Yet Paul speaks directly to them as moral agents accountable to God and worthy of reward. He lifts their daily obedience out of obscurity and anchors it in the presence of Christ Himself.

For the early church, this was radical. It meant that even unseen faithfulness had eternal value. Obedience was not rendered meaningless by injustice or lack of appreciation.

For believers across the centuries, this passage reinforces a central biblical theme: God's reward system is not dependent on human acknowledgment. The Lord sees what others overlook, and He promises to reward every good act done in faith, regardless of circumstance or response.

1 Corinthians 3:12–14

"If anyone builds on this foundation using gold, silver, costly stones . . . their work will be shown for what it is. . . . If what has been built survives, the builder will receive a reward."

Paul wrote to the Corinthian church, a spiritually gifted but deeply divided community. They were preoccupied with status, leadership personalities, and outward markers of success. Paul redirects their focus by reminding them that Christ alone is the foundation and that everything built upon Him will one day be tested.

The imagery of fire reflects a common biblical metaphor for divine evaluation. The issue is not whether one belongs to Christ—that foundation is settled—but whether one's work was done for God's glory or self-interest.

For the original audience, this passage confronted superficial spirituality and warned that not everything done in the name of faith would endure.

For believers throughout history, it establishes a sobering truth: All Christian living will be evaluated for quality, not just quantity. Works motivated by pride, control, or performance may look impressive now but they will not survive the refining fire. What is done in humility, love, and obedience will endure.

Colossians 3:23–24

"Whatever you do, work at it with all your heart, as working for the Lord . . . since you know that you will receive an inheritance from the Lord as a reward. It is the Lord Christ you are serving."

Paul wrote Colossians to a young church facing pressure from competing philosophies and distorted teachings. He repeatedly emphasizes Christ's supremacy, not only in doctrine, but in everyday life.

The phrase "whatever you do" intentionally removes any sacred/secular divide. For first-century believers, this meant that ordinary responsibilities like household duties, labor, or relationships were arenas of devotion. We worship in working. We magnify Him in marriage.

For the church across time, this passage affirms that Christian faith is lived out in the ordinary rhythms of life. Serving others faithfully is, in reality, service rendered to Christ

Himself. The promised inheritance reminds believers that God's rewards are not symbolic. They are real, future, and guaranteed.

Summary

Across these passages, a unified message emerges:

- Salvation is a free gift of grace (Ephesians 2:8–9).
- Faithfulness is personally accountable (Ephesians 6:7–8.)
- Reward is real, future, and Christ-centered (Colossians 3:24).
- Everyday obedience carries eternal weight (Colossians 3:17).

From Jesus' parables to Paul's letters, Scripture consistently teaches that God watches how His people live—not to condemn them but to reward faithfulness. Living with "well done" in mind is not about striving for approval. It is about stewarding what God has entrusted, in light of eternity.

This foundation prepares us to explore how these eternal truths are lived out practically, especially within marriage, where faithfulness is tested daily and often unseen.

Reflection

- ♦ In what ways have you viewed your daily efforts as disconnected from Christ's eternal reward?

- ♦ Have you been more concerned with how others respond to you than with how Christ sees your faithfulness?

- ♦ When you think about standing before Christ, do you sense you've been building with lasting materials (love, grace, humility) or temporary ones (control, pride, performance)?

- ♦ Do you believe that your ordinary, unseen acts of service—especially in your home—truly matter to God? Why or why not?

- ♦ How often do you let your choices be shaped by eternity rather than by immediate emotions, recognition, or results?

LIGHTBULB MOMENT #3

LIVING WITH "WELL DONE!" IN MIND

Practical Application

Now that you've reflected on what it means to live with eternity in view from a biblical perspective, take a few moments to apply this personally to your marriage.

The "*Aaaah!*" Moment

Think back to a gift you received that made you gasp with joy. That's a tiny, tiny echo of the joy we'll feel when Christ says, "Well done."

- How might that anticipation shape the way you serve, love, and forgive . . . knowing Jesus is watching?

Eternal Perspective in the Everyday

Your marriage carries eternal significance. Every act of love and respect matters to Christ, and it will not go unrewarded.

- What difference does it make to know that no faithful act is wasted, even when your spouse doesn't notice? How can you live with eternity in view?

I shared how my mother's final poem pointed to eternity just weeks before her death. She lived with heaven in view, and we can too, even in marriage.

- If someone were to read your final words, would they point to eternity? Would your marriage reflect that same eternal focus?

From Fairness to Faithfulness

A wife once said, "I stopped clinging to fairness and started clinging to faithfulness." That shift changed her marriage.

- How do you feel about her lightbulb moment in marriage?

- Which of these choices have marked your week? Because of Jesus . . .

  - ❑ *I can choose patience over irritation.*
  - ❑ *I can show respect even when feeling unheard.*
  - ❑ *I can pray instead of blame.*
  - ❑ *I can trust Him with outcomes.*

- What is your next step toward faithfulness?

Living for the Applause of Heaven

A husband said, "I stopped asking, 'Is she grateful?' and started asking, 'Is He pleased?'"

- How does that question reframe what success looks like in your marriage? What do you want Jesus to see in you that pleases Him?

Your marriage is a tool and a test to deepen and demonstrate your love and reverence for Jesus Christ. Every act of love and respect touches His heart, and it will not go unrewarded.

- What would it mean for you personally to shift from asking, "Is my spouse responding?" to asking, "Am I loving or respecting unto the Lord?"

LIGHTBULB MOMENT #4

THE HOLY WORD, NOT HOLLYWOOD

Biblical Foundation

From the beginning, God has called His people to be shaped by His truth—not the world's ideas. Scripture offers a radically different vision for love and life, one rooted in covenant, sacrifice, and holiness. Yet in today's culture, competing voices bombard us with counterfeit versions of love that look appealing but lack the depth and durability of God's design.

This Lightbulb Moment invites us to pause and ask: *Whose definition of truth are we trusting? Scripture or the screen? The way of Christ or the way of culture?*

Matthew 4:4

"Man shall not live on bread alone, but on every word that comes from the mouth of God."

Jesus reminds us that life is sustained not by what the world feeds us but by what God declares to be true. While culture promises satisfaction through pleasure, success, or romance, those things cannot nourish the soul. According to Jesus, only God's Word provides what is necessary for real life, real faithfulness, and lasting peace.

Reflection

- What does this word of Jesus reveal about what should be the primary focus of our life?

Hebrews 1:1–2

"God, after He spoke long ago to the fathers in the prophets in many portions and in many ways, in these last days has spoken to us in His Son" (NASB).

Scripture reveals a God who speaks. Our God is not silent. Through the prophets—and ultimately through His Son—God has made His will known. We are not left to guess what truth looks like; Jesus Himself is the final and authoritative revelation of God's heart. Though God speaks through David's poetry, the legislation of Moses, a donkey, an angel, a burning bush, a still, small voice, or through the few sentences or many of a prophet, what He has spoken is exactly what He intended to say.

Reflection

- Since God has spoken, regardless of the means of His choosing, then His Word is not optional but essential and carries authority that stands above personal preference, emotion, or culture. How does that challenge modern ideas of autonomy?

2 Peter 1:21

"For no prophecy was ever made by an act of human will, but men moved by the Holy Spirit spoke from God" (NASB).

This verse reminds us that Scripture did not originate in human insight or intention. Though God used human authors, the message itself was directed and carried along by the Holy Spirit. The authority of Scripture rests not in human wisdom but in divine initiative.

Reflection

- Since Scripture comes from God rather than human will, how should that shape the authority it holds in your life?

2 Timothy 3:16–17

"All Scripture is God-breathed and is useful for teaching, rebuking, correcting, and training in righteousness, so that the servant of God may be thoroughly equipped for every good work."

Where does Scripture come from? Paul answers: God Himself. For what purpose? God's Word instructs us in what is true, exposes what is wrong, redirects us on how to return to what is right, and forms godly-wise behavior in us.

Reflection

- How does Paul's description of Scripture call you to a more active response than simply reading words on a page?

- When was the last time God's Word taught, rebuked, corrected, or trained you? What good came from that?

John 17:17

"Sanctify them in the truth; Your word is truth" (NASB).

To *sanctify* is for God to claim someone as His own and shape them for holy use. Jesus prayed that this would occur through truth. God's truth. This truth is reality as God defines it, and God's Word is the means by which that reality is made known.

Reflection

- How does viewing truth as "reality as God defines it" affect the way you respond to the claim that everyone has their own truth?

- In those moments, how does God's Word anchor you?

Matthew 7:24, 26

"Therefore whosoever heareth these sayings of mine, and doeth them, I will liken him unto a wise man, which built his house upon a rock. . . . And every one that heareth these sayings of mine, and doeth them not, shall be likened unto a foolish man, which built his house upon the sand" (KJV).

This passage challenges the assumption that listening equals obedience. Jesus draws a clear line between passive hearing and active response. The difference determines the outcome.

Reflection

- What contrast does Jesus draw between those who merely listen and those who act on His words?

Key Thought

The carnal world scripts truth in the spiritual and moral realm as something to feel or invent; Scripture reveals truth as something to receive, trust, and obey.

LIGHTBULB MOMENT #4

THE HOLY WORD, NOT HOLLYWOOD

Practical Application

Permit me to ask: *Do you live by the Holy Word or by Hollywood?* Most of us want to say the "Holy Word," yet many of us are more influenced by the "reel" than we realize. Culture feeds us a steady diet of emotional and sexual fantasy, and if we're not grounded in God's truth, disappointment follows—not because our spouse failed but because we expected them to live up to a movie script.

I've seen it repeatedly. Good people—God's people—nearly walk away from something sacred not because of unfaithfulness but because they are unknowingly following a script that has little to do with Scripture.

Hollywood's Reel Love vs. God's Real Love

- On a scale of 1 to 10, how influenced are you by Hollywood's view of love?

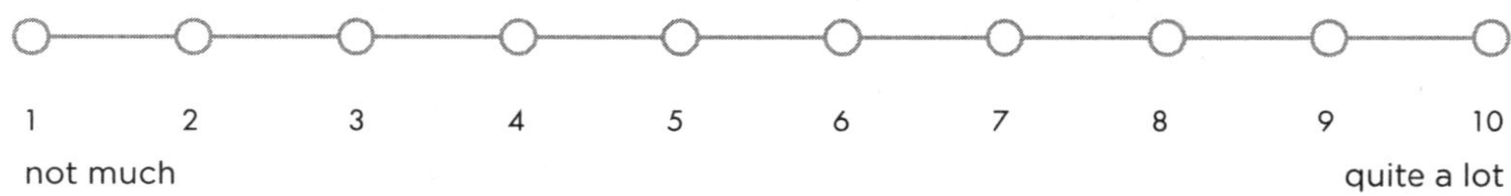

If you're on the higher end of that scale, ask yourself: *When was the last time I felt disappointed in my spouse? Could that disappointment be traced to a Hollywood-influenced expectation?*

One friend nearly ended her engagement after watching *Funny Girl*. The movie stirred a longing. Shouldn't love always feel electric? But then someone asked, "Are you chasing real love or reel love?" That question broke the illusion. She had confused Hollywood's version of love with God's. She stayed in the marriage, and later she and her husband mentored nearly ninety people into full-time ministry. What might her story have been otherwise?

- What is your reel love vs. real love moment? Write it here.

Reel Love vs. Real Love—The Shiny Lures of the World

One man shared how reel love nearly wrecked his marriage, not because his wife didn't love him, but because she didn't act like the seductive women in movies. He'd absorbed a fantasy: The ideal woman would always want sex, always initiate, always be adventuresome. Then he heard, "Your wife was designed to respond to love."

That moment changed him. He realized he'd been judging her by fiction instead of honoring her as God's gift.

We're all vulnerable to the world's shiny lures—appealing but deceptive ideals. Consider these five:

- **Possessions:** Do you believe more stuff makes your marriage feel more satisfying?
- **Status:** Are you chasing achievement to feel worth and respect?
- **Popularity:** Do social media couples make yours feel like you are missing out?
- **Sex:** Have your expectations been shaped more by media than by biblical love?
- **Romance:** Do you doubt your marriage when it doesn't feel magical?

♦ Whose voice are you following—the Holy Word or Hollywood?

Light vs. Darkness

Paul asked, "What fellowship can light have with darkness?" (2 Corinthians 6:14). The world makes darkness look glamorous through novels, shows, and online fantasy. But God calls us into His light.

Reflecting on the list above, let me ask, gently but honestly:

- Where have you chosen darkness over light?
- And what would it take to step into the light today?

♦ How would you answer these questions?

Checklist: Unrealistic Expectations in Marriage

Unrealistic expectations often show up differently in men and women. Check the following that apply and then reflect on how they are affecting your marriage.

Wives:

- ❑ You measure your relationship by novels or movies—expecting a husband who anticipates your needs with constant charm.
- ❑ You believe you should be soulmates and shouldn't have to work at marriage.
- ❑ You compare your marriage to social media and feel it falls short.
- ❑ You've daydreamed or formed emotional ties with someone else due to unmet needs.

Husbands:

- ❑ You pursue physical intimacy without emotional connection and feel hurt when she doesn't respond.
- ❑ You see sex as a trade—"I do X, so I should get Y."
- ❑ You've compared your sex life to Hollywood and feel disappointed.
- ❑ You've let sexual desire lead to fantasies or actions that erode trust.

♦ How is this impacting your marriage?

Is Marriage a Covenant to You?

Jesus said, "What God has joined together, let no one separate" (Matthew 19:6).

Marriage isn't just a contract. It's a sacred covenant. I shared in our session that God joined two together in covenant. Sex is sacred, reserved for marriage. Marriage mirrors both God's image and Christ's love for the church.

♦ Do you see your marriage as holy? If not, how would it change if you did?

Which Path Are You On?

The world says, "Follow your heart." Jesus says, "Follow Me." When push comes to shove, who are you listening to? The carnal world or the eternal Word? Jesus said, "Blessed are those who hear the word of God and follow it" (Luke 11:28 NASB).

- How would you answer this question?

Closing Thought

Everything you do in your marriage matters.

Every time you show love to your wife or respect to your husband, Jesus sees, and He will reward it.

That's not sentiment. That's Scripture: "Well done, good and faithful servant! . . . Come and share your master's happiness!" (Matthew 25:21).

Even if no one else sees, Jesus does. And He honors your faithfulness.

So let me ask once more: Will you live by the Holy Word or Hollywood?

Weekly Check-In

Sometime this week, after you and your spouse have both completed the personal studies, take about fifteen minutes to meet and reflect on your key takeaways. Use this time to share what encouraged you most.

Suggested Questions [PICK 2 TO 3]

Lightbulb Moment #3: Living with "Well Done!" in Mind

- What encouraged you most in the truth that your marriage carries eternal significance? Why?
- Was there a moment in this session that made you pause and think, *Wow—I hadn't thought of my marriage as something Jesus will reward*?
- Do you really believe that Christ notices and values your faithfulness, even in the small things?
- What's one thing—big or small—that you're doing together right now as husband and wife that, when you stand before Jesus, might lead Him to say, "Well done, good and faithful servant"?

Lightbulb Moment #4: The Holy Word, Not Hollywood

- In what ways have you grown in recognizing and rejecting Hollywood's version of love, romance, or intimacy?
- Where have you seen the fruit of following Jesus rather than following your emotions or cultural pressure?
- What's one belief you've realigned with Scripture that has brought more peace, joy, or intimacy into your marriage?
- Were there moments in this session—or in Scripture—that deepened your confidence that God's Word is your best guide for love and marriage?
- In what ways have you and your spouse intentionally guarded your hearts from worldly messages and stood firm on biblical truth?
- Looking back, what's one area where you now say, "Thank You, Lord, we're no longer believing that lie"?

Looking Ahead

Read **chapters 5–6** in *Lightbulb Moments in Marriage* before your next group. Use the space below to write down anything from those chapters that stands out, challenges you, or encourages your heart.

BEFORE GROUP MEETING	Read chapters 5–6 in *Lightbulb Moments in Marriage* Read the Welcome section (page 50)
GROUP MEETING	Discuss the Connect questions (page 50) Watch the video teaching for session 3 and take notes (pages 50–53) Engage in a Group Discussion on the material (pages 54–55) Couples have a Husband and Wife Discussion (page 55) Close in Group Prayer (page 56)
PERSONAL STUDY	
LIGHTBULB MOMENT #5: BIBLICAL FOUNDATION	Complete the Biblical Foundation personal study for Lightbulb Moment #5 (pages 58–63)
LIGHTBULB MOMENT #5: PRACTICAL APPLICATION	Complete the Practical Application personal study for Lightbulb Moment #5 (pages 64–67)
LIGHTBULB MOMENT #6: BIBLICAL FOUNDATION	Complete the Biblical Foundation personal study for Lightbulb Moment #6 (pages 68–73)
LIGHTBULB MOMENT #6: PRACTICAL APPLICATION	Complete the Practical Application personal study for Lightbulb Moment #6 (pages 74–78)
WEEKLY CHECK-IN	Connect with your spouse during the week to discuss your key insights from this session (page 79)
BEFORE NEXT WEEK	Read chapters 7–8 in *Lightbulb Moments in Marriage*

SESSION THREE

OUR CLARITY AND OUR HARMONY

LIGHTBULB #5:

Understanding Each Other, Not Just Talking

Speaking more doesn't fix confusion—true communication means understanding each other's "pink" and "blue" language.

LIGHTBULB #6:

Same Team, Same Goal, Different Plays

Your differences allow you to brainstorm and find the best route to the same destination.

Welcome [READ ON YOUR OWN]

You will often hear people say that communication is the key to marriage. This makes sense at one level. After all, couples do have to speak to each other for any understanding to occur. But it's a misperception that *more* communication in marriage always leads to *better* communication. There comes a point when just talking more doesn't necessarily bring greater clarity.

Lightbulb Moment #5 focuses on *clarity*. You and your spouse can use the same words but mean different things. Without mutual understanding of each other's "pink" and "blue" language, words can feel unloving or disrespectful. Even well-worded sentences can trigger the Crazy Cycle if heard through a different lens.

Lightbulb Moment #6 brings in *harmony*. You're not opponents; you're teammates. You likely share the same goals but have different approaches. Harmony grows when you lean into your differences, meet calmly at the "whiteboard," and work it out together. This prevents the Crazy Cycle and builds real resolution.

Connect [5 TO 15 MINUTES]

Get the session started by choosing one or both of the following questions to discuss:

- Have you ever needed to communicate with someone who didn't speak your language—maybe while traveling and meeting someone from another culture? What did you do to try and be understood?

— *or* —

- Have you and your spouse ever tried to solve a problem together—maybe assemble furniture, plan a trip, or pack for a move—both aiming for the same goal but using completely different strategies? What happened, and what did you learn about your differences?

Watch [30 TO 40 MINUTES]

As you watch this video session, I invite you not only to follow the teaching but also to reflect personally on the stories I share about Sarah and me. These aren't just illustrations—they're windows into a real, sometimes messy, often hilarious, and always sacred journey we've walked together. As you watch, I hope you see glimpses of your own story in ours. And, more importantly, I pray these lightbulb moments become part of your journey too. Use the outline to follow along with the teaching, and then jot down key takeaways.

Outline: Lightbulb Moments #5 & #6

I. Lightbulb Moment #5—Our Clarity: Understanding Each Other, Not Just Talking

- General Principles
  - Everyone says communication is key, but the real key is mutual understanding. I could speak perfect Spanish, but if my wife only speaks German, she won't get it.
  - The same words don't mean the same thing. " have nothing to wear" means nothing *new* to her but nothing *clean* to him.
  - Ask, "Have we argued where the issue wasn't the issue?" That's often a clue that love and respect needs are going unmet.
- Personal Story: The Jean Jacket and Contact Lens
  - One Christmas, Sarah gave me a handmade jean jacket. I said "thank you" once. She thought I didn't like it. Her family repeated appreciation; mine didn't. I felt misunderstood and disrespected. I deflated.
  - Then came the contact lens story. I used juice glasses as cases; she unknowingly drank one of the contacts. I called her out in front of my parents. The real issue wasn't the contact, it was my obvious frustration with her, and she felt unloved. She deflated.
- The Crazy Cycle
  - I asked 7,000 people: "In conflict, do you feel unloved or disrespected?" 83% of men said disrespected, 72% of women said unloved. That's revealing.
  - Ephesians 5:33 commands husbands to love and wives to respect. When we violate that, it's like stepping on each other's air hose.
  - She needs love like air. He needs respect like oxygen. Step on that, and we both deflate.

II. Lightbulb Moment #6—Our Harmony: Same Team, Same Goal, Different Plays

- General Principles
  - You're not opponents. You're teammates. The goal is shared; the method may differ. For example, Sarah and I debated flying or taking the train to visit family in Paris. The "how" created tension, not the "why."
  - This principle applies to intimacy too. First Corinthians 7:5 reminds couples to reach mutual agreement. Emotional and physical connection isn't a power struggle.
  - Most conflict isn't about right or wrong but about preference differences. When we recognize shared goals, we can move from battling to brainstorming.

S.T.E.P.: A Practical Framework for Emotional and Sexual Oneness

Let me give you a practical tool. I call it S.T.E.P., and it can help any couple come to mutual agreement, especially in sensitive areas like emotional and sexual connection.

- **S** **S**tate the issue clearly. Just the issue. Don't throw in everything else. For example: "How do we find mutual satisfaction emotionally and sexually in our marriage?"
- **T** **T**alk about your perspective honestly and gently. Express how you feel, but with kindness and goodwill. No attacking, no power plays.
- **E** **E**valuate your shared vision. Remind yourselves: same team, same goal. You both want emotional connection. You both want sexual satisfaction. You both want to honor Christ.
- **P** **P**lan forward using the 5 Ws + H: *Who? What? When? Where? Why? How?* This is where creative alternatives can emerge, what we refer to as the "third option."

- How to Keep the Issue to the Issue
    - Whiteboard Principle—Visualize a whiteboard. Write only the facts. Don't start with emotions or personal attacks. Keep the issue to the issue.
    - Check the Air Hose—Ask, "Are we getting a bit emotional, stepping on each other's air hoses to our love and respect tanks?"
    - Catch the Whiteboard Before It Falls—When the conversation starts getting too emotional, someone needs to say, "Wait, this isn't about the topic/issue anymore." Redirect to the real issue before feelings get out of control and each feels unloved and disrespected. Return to the facts of the issue.
    - Call a Timeout—What if it gets way too emotional? For example, when a man hits 99 BPM (beats per minute), he's flooded and in warrior mode. Take fifteen minutes. Regroup. Come back better prepared to address the issue.
    - Push Reset—Even if it all went sideways, start over. Say, "Can we hit reset and calmly return to the facts? Let's try again, with both of our interests in mind."

Notes

Write down the concepts that grab your heart. Remember these lightbulb moments aren't just information—they're meant to bring transformation in your marriage.

Notes

Group Discussion [30 TO 45 MINUTES]

Pick your adventure from these questions!

Group Reflection Prompts

1. I shared how "I have nothing to wear" can mean *nothing new* or *nothing clean*. Same words, different meanings. Where have you seen this kind of misunderstanding in your marriage? How has assuming meaning, rather than seeking understanding, created tension?
2. I asked the question, "What is the issue when the issue isn't the issue?" Can you recall a conflict where the original topic disappeared and something deeper surfaced?
3. Looking back, do you think feelings of being **unloved** or **disrespected** were underneath that moment? (I am not saying that you were, in fact, unloved or disrespected, only that you felt that way at the moment.)
4. In the stories I told of the jean jacket and the contact lens, neither was really about a jacket or a contact lens but about a deflated spirit. Which part of those stories resonated the most with you, and why? Have you experienced a moment where your spouse's reaction surprised you because you didn't realize what they were feeling, though you observed them deflate?
5. Based on Ephesians 5:33, I described the Crazy Cycle: *Without love, she reacts without respect. Without respect, he reacts without love.* When conflict arises, which side of the cycle do you tend to experience first—feeling unloved or disrespected? How does recognizing the Crazy Cycle help you name what's really happening instead of escalating it?
6. I explained that she needs love like air, and he needs respect like oxygen. How can you tell when your spouse's "air hose" is being stepped on? What might it look like to respond with awareness instead of reacting defensively in that moment?
7. I shared the example of deciding whether to fly or take the train to Paris. Same destination, different routes. What's a current "gray area" in your marriage where you want the same outcome but disagree on how to get there? (Stay light-hearted!) How does remembering that you're on the same team change the tone of that conversation?
8. From 1 Corinthians 7:5, I emphasized that God calls couples to *agreement*, not *domination*, especially in emotional and sexual intimacy. Why do you think it's easier to avoid these conversations than to brainstorm together? What would it look like to pursue a *win-win* instead of waiting for one person to give in?

Note: This is your call as a group, but in the teaching I willingly risk surfacing a tough topic of emotional and sexual connection. First Corinthians 7:1–5 expects believers to address this topic, so here we go—if you so decide. But let's tread with humility, mutual honor, and a commitment to seek Christ together as we discreetly navigate this. These conversations are not to shame or pressure but to foster understanding, unity, and healing among Christ-followers. These Scriptures were publicly read in the assembly, and the Lord expected the body of Christ to seek godly and wise ways to apply His revelation among husbands and wives, especially since Satan prioritizes this issue.

---

9. I introduced practical tools like the whiteboard, checking air hoses, timeouts, and the S.T.E.P. process. Which of these tools do you think would help your marriage the most right now? What's one small step you could take this week to keep the issue the issue and protect your connection?
10. What was your biggest lightbulb moment from this session?

Husband and Wife Discussion [5 TO 15 MINUTES]

Now take a few minutes to talk privately with your spouse. Focus on connection, not correction; encouragement, not exhortation. Revisit any question from the group time or use one or two of these prompts to go deeper:

Conversation Starters

1. Did someone share something in the group discussion that really encouraged you?
2. When have you seen the Crazy Cycle in action in your relationship? (We all get on it. Sarah and I still do.)
3. What's one small step you could take this week to stop the cycle when it starts?
4. Was it a good reminder to make sure to say, "Let's keep the issue to the issue" to prevent the Crazy Cycle?
5. Could asking, "Am I stepping on your air hose?" help or hinder a moment of marital tension?
6. How might you apply the S.T.E.P. model to a minor issue currently in front of you?

Identify something small and manageable, an area where you could reasonably find agreement and experience an early win. I emphasize "minor" because success here builds confidence and goodwill. If emotional or sexual intimacy feels like a major issue right now, that conversation may be best postponed until trust and connection are strengthened. And, in such cases, defer to the one who feels more vulnerable, not out of passivity but as an act of love, humility, and Christlike regard (Philippians 2:3–4).

Group Prayer [5 TO 10 MINUTES]

Close your time by praying together. Thank God for the gift of understanding, not just information.

Ask for the humility to recognize when you've stepped on each other's air hose. Pray for help in catching yourselves before the Crazy Cycle spins out of control.

Invite the Holy Spirit to help you use tools like S.T.E.P., timeouts, and reset moments to protect your unity.

Ask for grace to be quick to listen, slow to speak, and eager to forgive.

SESSION THREE

PERSONAL STUDY

So far in this study, we've been laying the foundation. We've been focusing not on self-help beliefs but on what we believe about God, His Word, and how He views us: our identity in Christ, His presence in our marriage, and the eternal reward He promises.

That foundation matters. Once we understand what's true about God and what He's doing in us, we're better prepared to live that out, especially in our marriages.

Starting with this session, we began shifting to the practical skills that bring clarity and harmony with our spouse. It's not enough to know the truth. We have to live it. And that shows up in how we speak, listen, and respond when the Crazy Cycle starts spinning.

As you move through this personal study, ask God to open your eyes to what He wants to show you, especially in your relationship. Reflect deeply and write your responses. These notes will help center your thoughts when you talk with your spouse.

If you're reading *Lightbulb Moments in Marriage*, first read chapters 5–6. They go hand-in-hand with this session, especially around understanding each other and staying united, even when your approaches differ. Let's keep going.

LIGHTBULB MOMENT #5

UNDERSTANDING EACH OTHER, NOT JUST TALKING

Biblical Foundation

Ephesians 5:33

"However, let each one of you love his wife as himself, and let the wife see that she respects her husband" (ESV).

This verse helped define what I call the Crazy Cycle: Without love, she reacts without respect; without respect, he reacts without love. Around and around it goes.

Paul doesn't simply say, "Love one another." He's more specific. Husbands are commanded to love, and wives are commanded to respect. This is not because only women need love or only men need respect. Scripture affirms that both are essential (see 1 Peter 3:7; Titus 2:4). But Ephesians 5:33 highlights our primary felt needs and what often fuels our negative reactions during conflict.

When a wife says, "I need respect," I agree with that statement. But I also note that no romantic movie ends with the hero declaring, "I want to respect you for the rest of my life." The cultural script for women is love. Still, when a husband acts in a disrespectful way, a wife eventually pushes back and says, "How can you say you love me when you treat me this way?" What she's really saying is, "Real love does not dishonor."

Husbands, on the other hand, usually don't say, "I feel unloved." More often they say, "You're not respecting me." And the wife might respond, "I do love you, but right now I don't respect you." Love and respect are not interchangeable, but both are vital.

In tense moments, we tend to default to our reflex needs. When she feels unloved, her response often sounds disrespectful. When he feels disrespected, his response often comes across as unloving. This is the Crazy Cycle—and Ephesians 5:33 offers the remedy.

It's important to clarify this verse is not an endorsement of an unloving, authoritarian man, nor is it a demand that a wife tolerate sin by respecting the husband as the patriarch who does no wrong. Scripture never commands women to enable narcissism or sin. In fact, women in the Bible had far more agency than many realize (see Mark 7:10–12; 1 Corinthians 7:10–11). Paul's instruction on respect is not male control.

With great fascination, I realized that Peter, in another passage, lands solely on respect and honor and says nothing of love. Peter says that a husband is to "show honor" (1 Peter 3:7) and a wife is to show "respectful conduct" (3:1–2). In other words, respect is not about the husband exercising dominance but both showing mutual, unconditional respect toward the other's demeanor.

Ephesians 5:33 helps couples name what's really happening beneath the surface. It helps them to pause and ask, "What's the real issue here?" Often, the tension isn't really about the topic at hand. The deeper issue is how we're making each other feel in the moment. Unloved. Disrespected. We must not treat this as a take-it-or-leave-it psychological idea. It is not outdated or culturally biased. This is God's revelation (see Ephesians 3:4–6) on what each spouse typically needs during conflict.

When a husband realizes his wife needs to feel his love, especially during disagreement, he will begin to adjust his tone and manner. He won't stop speaking truth, but he'll speak it with warmth and humility. Likewise, when a wife understands her husband needs to feel respected—not for his performance, but for who he is—she will choose her words and attitude carefully, even while sharing hard things.

In short, a husband cannot communicate truth while being harsh or cold. And a wife cannot express her heart well through contempt or criticism. This is about who we are called to be before God, not about who our spouse fails to be.

Tone matters. Love matters. Respect matters. When we speak with love and respect, especially when it's hardest, we create the best possible conditions for meaningful and restorative communication.

For a Husband on His Communication

1 Peter 3:7

"Likewise, husbands, live with your wives in an understanding way, showing honor to the woman as the weaker vessel, since they are heirs with you of the grace of life, so that your prayers may not be hindered" (ESV).

Beyond the marriage relationship, Peter makes it clear: When a husband refuses to live with his wife in an understanding way as the Christ figure in the home, he will find that Christ Himself will not respond to him with understanding (so to speak). If a husband won't listen to his wife's heart and requests, the Lord won't listen to his heart and requests. Why such strong language? I believe it's because the Lord knows men get this. Most men, upon reflection, say to themselves, *Fair is fair. If I don't honor her, why should the Lord honor me?*

Peter's instruction here isn't vague. It's a command to study your wife, to make a lifelong commitment to know her inner world. Communication isn't always easy, but God first calls a husband to listen, observe, and reflect before he reacts. He needs to understand that his wife processes conflict through a different emotional lens. She's not wrong; she's different.

Understanding that difference, and trying to understand where she is coming from on an issue, not only honors her but also make a husband's prayer life more effective.

The phrase "weaker vessel" has often been misunderstood, as if Peter meant women are inferior. He didn't. Women aren't lesser, but they do have vulnerabilities that differ from a man's. When a man says, "No one could ever understand you, and I'm not going to honor you as my equal," she feels dismissed and defeated. The message she absorbs is that who she is doesn't matter. In a remarkable way, Peter and the feminist movement agree. Women long to be understood and honored as equals.

Instead of rejecting Peter's words, we should recognize how forward-thinking they truly are. He calls husbands to lead with honor and understanding. And this matters so much to God that He warns, if a husband dishonors his wife, his prayers will be hindered.

So, what's Peter saying here? He's telling husbands:

- Your wife isn't beneath you but is your spiritual equal.
- Don't treat her with indifference or condescension.
- Study her. Seek to understand her.
- Show her honor as one who will receive all that you inherit in heaven from Jesus.
- God is listening, so how you treat your wife determines whether He listens to you.

Given this, here are questions to ask in considering how to understand and honor her:

- "How do we make this a win for both of us so both of us advance our healthy self-interests?"
- "What would a solution look like that works for both of us, not just me?"
- "Can you help me understand what you need here? I want to support you without losing myself either."
- "I know what I'd prefer, but what feels fair to you in all this?"
- "I don't want this to feel like I'm pushing my way through. What do *you* think would work for *us*?"

For a Wife on Her Communication

1 Peter 3:1–2

"Likewise, wives, be subject to your own husbands, so that even if some do not obey the word, they may be won without a word by the conduct of their wives, when they see your respectful and pure conduct" (ESV).

Up front, we need to acknowledge a difficult truth. When a wife tries to win the heart of her husband, two things often happen. First, she may speak in ways that sound disrespectful to him, even if that is not her intent. At times, she may speak this way inadvertently, and at other times intentionally, especially if she feels he does not deserve respect.

Second, she may act in ways that appear disrespectful. Researchers at the University of Washington have identified physical expressions of contempt that communicate deep negativity, including a sour face, rolling eyes, dark stares, pointing fingers, sighing, hands on the hips, and "that look." These gestures often communicate more loudly than words and can quickly shut a husband down. As his anger and harshness are to her, so her gestures of contempt are to him.

Winning a husband "without a word" sounds passive or confusing to many wives, especially when they are dealing with a husband who seems spiritually shut down, emotionally distant, or self-absorbed. But "without a word" does not mean she plays a game of charades. Rather, it means she refrains from certain approaches: nagging, lecturing, shaming, parenting her husband, or manipulating him through guilt, sarcasm, or threats.

Peter's instruction is not about silencing the wife's voice. It is about protecting the tone and timing that give her voice influence. This kind of restraint does not come from weakness but from spiritual strength. It means she speaks less so that when she does speak, her words carry more weight.

From decades of ministry, I have observed that wives process issues verbally. Talking helps them process pain, pursue connection, and gain clarity. Silence often feels like distance, and distance feels like rejection. Right now, I know of two wives who are physically separated from their husbands. One husband is bitter and damaged property; the other is addicted to pornography. Both women long, deep in their core, to reconnect with their husbands. If either man were to reach out with humility and remorse, these wives would eagerly welcome the opportunity to talk at length about what he feels and what she feels. For them, talking is not about control but about closeness, resolution, and reconciliation. When the door opens, even slightly, they step through it to talk. Why wouldn't you?

At the same time, both confess their first instinct is to confront their husband's failings, and to do so with negative, disrespectful words. One drafted a scathing text, which she did not send, as she realized the next day it would not have won his heart but put him on the defensive as a complete failure. The other intended to point out to her husband, "You have been mean and nasty for forty years." Yes, true enough. But, I shared, if he hears only that he is the disease, how can he hear the deepest cry of your heart that you need him to be the cure?

When Peter instructs a wife to win her husband "without a word," he is not commanding total silence. Nor is he telling her to suppress her conscience. Peter himself witnessed the danger of silence in Acts 5:1–11, when Ananias and Sapphira conspired to lie to the Holy Spirit. Peter gave Sapphira a chance to speak truthfully, but she repeated the lie and suffered the consequences. Peter expected Sapphira to respectfully say to Ananias, "I will not go along with this plan." A wife is never called to enable sin or violate her conscience.

So when an issue is moral or spiritual, she must speak with courage and clarity, but always with a respectful demeanor and respectful word choice. She might say, "I married you because I believe in you. I am for you, not against you. I believe in God's call on your life. I see myself as your team player helping you in that calling. But I cannot agree with this. I trust God to help you hear my respect, even as I share something difficult."

This kind of language honors her husband's dignity while still drawing a clear boundary. It does not flatter or enable wrongdoing. It calls him upward.

At the same time, not every disagreement is a moral failure. Often it is simply a clash of preferences. In those moments, it is easy for a wife to believe she is right, he is wrong, and to push harder with words. But when she crosses from influence into control, or from lover into mother, the Crazy Cycle begins. A barrage of words rarely produces change. It more often produces resistance. Instead, she might say:

- "Can you help me understand what you're thinking?"
- "Could we both pray and revisit this tomorrow?"
- "I want to support you, but I also hope you'll consider what I'm seeing. Maybe we can find a solution that works for both of us."

If her husband does not respond as she hopes, Peter gives her four anchors. She is to entrust herself to God who judges justly, as Jesus did (1 Peter 2:23). She is to remember that God sees her suffering when she does what is right (2:19–20). She is to know that her gentle and quiet spirit is precious in God's sight (3:4). And she is to humble herself under God's mighty hand, trusting that He will lift her up in due time (5:6–7).

Communication does not succeed simply because we say everything on our minds. Peter himself once blurted out words without understanding what he was saying, as recorded in Mark 9 and Luke 9. Later, he learned a better way. Now he is passing that wisdom on, calling wives to a form of communication marked by respect, self-control, and godly influence that God honors.

Reflection

For the Husband:

♦ Ask yourself before speaking to your wife, "Is what I'm about to say going to sound loving or unloving to her? Will she feel understood and honored?" In your opinion, how would asking that question improve communication, strengthen your relationship, and help your concerns actually be heard?

For the Wife:

- Ask yourself before speaking to your husband, "Is what I'm about to say going to sound respectful or disrespectful to him?" In your opinion, how would asking that question improve communication, strengthen your relationship, and help your concerns actually be heard, especially since your husband knows you love him?

LIGHTBULB MOMENT #5

UNDERSTANDING EACH OTHER, NOT JUST TALKING

Practical Application

You don't need more talking. You need more mutual understanding.

Seeing Differently: Pink and Blue Lenses

I often say, "Not wrong, just different."

A wife says, "I have nothing to wear," meaning she has nothing *new*. A husband says the same, meaning he has nothing *clean*. Same phrase, very different meaning. That's how miscommunication happens. We speak English, but with different filters.

In this session, I explained how men and women can say the same words but decode entirely different meanings. That's why more talking doesn't always help. If you don't decode the lens your spouse hears through, you escalate confusion.

We often assume the solution is more talk. But without decoding or clarifying, more words just create more misunderstanding.

- When have you both said the same thing but meant different things?
- What's a recent moment where you misunderstood each other despite good intentions?
- How could remembering the "lens" help you clarify next time?
- How might "not wrong, just different" reframe your spouse's words?

Goodwill Interpretation: Giving the Benefit of the Doubt

Another theme: Interpret your spouse through goodwill, not suspicion.

Too often we assume the worst in our spouse. But what if the clumsy words or awkward tone weren't an attack but a misfire?

Couples who assume goodwill stop defensiveness before it starts.

- ♦ When did you last assume the worst, then realize it was a misunderstanding?
- ♦ How would assuming goodwill change your tone?

Stepping on Air Hoses

Love and respect are like air hoses. A wife connects to her love tank, a husband to his respect tank. When one steps on the other's hose, even unintentionally, emotional deflation happens. Tone, eye rolls, or quick replies can crush the spirit, even if no harm was meant.

Often, it's not what was said but how it felt. The tone or glance says more than the words.

- ♦ What reactions from your spouse feel like "air hose stepping"?
- ♦ What do you do that might deflate your spouse?
- ♦ What's one cue you could both use to signal gently, "You stepped on my air hose"?

Breaking the Crazy Cycle

Without love, she reacts without respect. Without respect, he reacts without love. The Crazy Cycle spins faster.

Most think the conflict is about the topic. And sometimes it is. But if you ignore what's causing emotional deflation, you miss the heart of the matter. Often:

- She feels unloved.
- He feels disrespected.

When emotional needs go unrecognized, we keep spinning. The issue isn't always the issue. We break the cycle not by fixing the topic but by addressing the heart need—love and respect in the midst of disagreement.

- Have you ever argued about one thing but then realized the pain came from feeling unloved or disrespected?

- What triggers those feelings for you?

- What's something your spouse means well by but that lands wrong?

- What phrase or action could help you interrupt the Crazy Cycle?

When the Issue Isn't the Issue: Feeling Disrespected

I shared a story in the teaching where Sarah gave me a handmade jean jacket. I thanked her, once. Because I didn't say "thank you" multiple times, she questioned my sincerity. I felt she was questioning my integrity.

Soon I shut down emotionally. I didn't have the words to say, "I feel disrespected." But that's exactly what I felt. I never doubted her love. But at some point, it wasn't about the jacket. The real issue was that I felt disrespected—as though she thought I was dishonest.

- Can you recall a disagreement where the real issue was a feeling of disrespect?

When the Issue Isn't the Issue: Feeling Unloved

Then there was the time Sarah accidentally drank my contact lens, which was soaking in a juice glass on the back of the toilet. I got angry, right in front of my parents. That embarrassed her.

It wasn't about the contact anymore. It was about how I treated her. Yes, she might say she feels disrespected, but over time, that morphs into a question of love: "How can you keep treating me this way and say you love me?"

- Can you remember a conflict where the underlying issue was feeling unloved?

Real-Life Couple Misunderstandings: Intent vs. Interpretation

In the teaching, I shared how easily we misinterpret good intentions. Here are real-life examples where neither spouse meant harm but misunderstanding took over.

Example #1: The Fix-It Husband
She says she's overwhelmed. He offers a solution. She hears, "You don't care how I feel." He means, "I care, so I want to fix it."

Example #2: The Supportive Wife
She points out a missed detail. He hears, "You're criticizing me again." She meant, "I'm supporting you."

Example #3: The Joking Husband
Tension rises. He jokes to break it. She hears, "You're dismissing me." He meant, "I hate this tension; I want us to laugh."

♦ Have you ever tried to help but your spouse misread your intent?

♦ What's a story where you both meant well but missed each other?

Resetting After Conflict: Using Appropriate Humor

In one argument, Sarah grabbed a copy of *Love & Respect* and asked, "What would you say to a husband treating his wife like you are right now?" I said, "That's not fair—I just write about this. I don't do it." That moment of humor broke the tension and helped us reconnect.

♦ What phrase, inside joke, or memory could help you reset emotionally during conflict?

♦ Here are some key reset phrases for your marriage toolbox. These aren't magic, but they can help restore connection when conflict rises:

- "Let's keep the issue the issue."
- "Are we stepping on each other's air hose?"
- "Let's take a time out and revisit this in fifteen minutes."
- "Let's push reset and try again with calmer hearts."

Which of these feels natural to you?

♦ Could you both agree to use one of these phrases the next time things escalate?

LIGHTBULB MOMENT #6

SAME TEAM, SAME GOAL, DIFFERENT PLAYS

Biblical Foundation

In every marriage, a husband and wife long for the same summit: intimate connection. They want emotional, physical, and spiritual oneness. They're not adversaries but teammates, both moving toward closeness, longing for love and respect. Yet the trail each prefers is often very different.

One path winds gently upward, with scenic overlooks, soft switchbacks, and quiet canopy. This is the emotional path, marked by reflection, safety, and shared presence. It is typically the wife's path. She finds connection through conversation, tenderness, and eye contact. Emotional intimacy draws her to sexual closeness.

The other path is steeper and more direct, cutting through rugged terrain with bursts of vertical gain. This is the sexual path: physical, focused, driven by momentum. It is typically the husband's path, and for him, intimacy begins with passion and desire. Physical connection opens him to emotional vulnerability.

Neither trail is wrong. They are simply different God-designed routes to the same destination.

Here's the key: She reaches emotional and sexual connection by starting emotionally. He reaches sexual and emotional connection by starting sexually.

Same summit. Different climb.

But this often goes unseen. She longs to be desired, but not when it feels like sex is the goal and she's the means. She needs emotional safety before offering her body.

He longs to be close. Not just physically, but as best friends. But not when every conversation feels like correction or his needs are brushed aside as selfish. When he feels sexually rejected, he shuts down emotionally.

What happens as a result? They both begin reacting to rejection. She resists the physical when she doesn't feel known. He withdraws emotionally when he feels unwanted. They drift apart, not because they lack love and respect, but because they forget that they climb differently.

The truth? They're on the same team, striving for the same summit: emotional and sexual oneness. She's seeking emotional connection that leads to sexual closeness. He's seeking sexual closeness that leads to emotional connection.

Both routes are sacred. Both must be honored.

The point isn't whose path is better but recognizing that love and respect walk hand in hand and choosing the other's trail isn't loss but intimacy. The shared climax.

But what happens when, on a given night, only one trail can be chosen? Trouble. And Scripture affirms this tension is real.

1 Corinthians 7:28

"If you marry, you have not sinned. . . . Yet such people as yourselves will have trouble in this life, and I am trying to spare you" (NASB).

I often quote this verse at marriage conferences. People laugh, especially when I suggest posting it on the refrigerator. Paul isn't being cynical. He's being honest. Trouble comes not because something is wrong with your marriage but because something sacred is being formed between "pink" and "blue."

This is God's classroom. Those "Why don't you get me?" moments aren't failures; they're invitations to grow. The tension isn't your enemy; it's the terrain God uses to teach two people how to walk as one without either disappearing. You don't need to fear the difference. You need to learn to name it and mature through it.

Reflection

- What kind of "trouble" has God used to grow you in your marriage?

- How does this verse reshape your view of conflict and connection?

These special challenges emerge not just because of our pink and blue differences. The Lord actually designed holy trouble in the bedroom by giving both husband and wife final say.

1 Corinthians 7:4–5

"The wife does not have authority over her own body, but the husband does; and likewise the husband also does not have authority over his own body, but the wife does. Stop depriving one another, except by agreement for a time" (NASB).

In the marriage bed, God gives equal authority to both husband and wife! So, does he decide? Does she decide? Yes! Thus the holy, God-given challenges. Sarah and I cannot make decisions about intimacy unless we *both* agree. The phrase "except by agreement" may be one of the most profound truths on marriage in all of Scripture.

Neither the husband nor wife can override the other. Final say must come through mutual agreement, not pressure. But when they don't agree, how do they move forward?

Practical application is fitting right here. You cannot control the outcomes in your spouse, but you can control your actions and reactions to your spouse. Sarah and I are still in process, but we seek to apply 1 Corinthians 7:4–5, 28 with these truths in front of us as our same destination—knowing we have different routes.

My Mindset

- I recognize that vulnerability looks different for each of us.
- Though my needs matter, I realize not every "yes" will come right now.
- I reframe unmet needs as opportunities to grow in patience and humility.
- I honor my spouse's "no" today as much as I value their "yes" and I let my humility enable me to make an appeal to connect tomorrow.
- I don't keep score against my spouse but I seek to be fair, which research refers to as "reciprocity."

My Commitment

- When my need is unmet on any particular day, I don't turn on my spouse with hostility or contempt.
- I don't weaponize past refusals to punish present moments.
- I take rejection to the Lord instead of taking it out on my spouse.
- I avoid cornering my spouse into decisions during emotionally charged moments.

My Approach

- I lead with love and respect in obedience to Christ, even when in the short-term I feel deprived.
- I act in goodwill and trust my spouse has goodwill, though we differ today.
- I express appreciation for effort even when the outcomes fall short.

My Speech

- I guard my tone and volume when expressing a need.
- I pause to ask, "What does connection look like for you tonight?"
- I express my desires without making demands.
- I first convey my intent to meet my spouse's needs before I humbly appeal to them to meet mine.
- I stay lighthearted and playful, though I could take offense and claim rejection.

This can feel unfair on any given day, but the Lord calls us to trust Him with this mindset, commitment, approach, and speech based on 1 Corinthians 7:4–5, 28.

Reflection

- Looking at these four areas—**My Mindset**, **My Commitment**, **My Approach**, and **My Speech**—which one best reflects how you are responding to your spouse right now?

Matthew 19:4

"Have you not read that He who created them from the beginning made them male and female?" (NASB).

Jesus takes us back to God's original design: male and female. Equal in worth, different by design. He's not promoting sameness. He's affirming difference and calling it good.

This is the foundation of the "pink" and "blue" lens analogy. Many couples stumble by expecting their spouse to think, feel, or communicate the same way they do. But God didn't create androgyny. He created difference. And difference is not deficiency.

You've heard it before: "Not wrong, just different." Your spouse sees through a different lens not because they're flawed but because they're wired that way. The sooner we honor that reality, the sooner we stop trying to fix what God never asked us to change.

Here is where many couples end up misunderstanding each other when it comes to male-and-female needs and their emotional and sexual desires. After intimacy, husbands and wives often misread each other due to different wiring. For many men, sex builds emotional closeness. He may feel deeply connected after their precious moment, so he heads to the garage to putter around. To him, this isn't detachment but contentment.

She, however, often seeks connection through conversation, so his going to the garage may feel like rejection. At the same time, when she lies next to him after their sexual moment, her mind quickly shifts to practical tasks, like planning groceries. He may assume that she wasn't truly engaged, when in fact she was present, pleased to give herself. But she moves on to her family concerns, as mothers do.

Both need to meet halfway. He can offer simple reassurance and not interpret her response negatively after intimacy. She can trust his silence doesn't mean indifference and reassure him the moment was most enjoyable.

Reflection

- Where has your spouse's emotional and sexual wiring frustrated you, when actually it might be part of God's design of them?

- What "fix" emotionally and sexually have you tried to make that may be rooted in misunderstanding and not truth?

- How could honoring your spouse's different emotional and sexual needs transform your next misunderstanding and frustration?

1 Corinthians 7:10–11

"But to the married I give instructions, not I, but the Lord, that the wife is not to leave her husband (but if she does leave, she must remain unmarried, or else be reconciled to her husband), and that the husband should not divorce his wife" (NASB).

Critics sometimes label the Bible chauvinistic, but Paul's instruction here is profoundly countercultural and deeply hopeful. The wife is not silenced or erased. She has agency. She may separate. She has a voice. But the aim is never abandonment. It is reconciliation.

Paul is unmistakable: Separation is not the goal; reconciliation is. Even when pain, disappointment, emotional neglect, or sexual frustration have wounded the heart deeply, God's call is not for couples to give up but to find a way back. Both husband and wife are addressed. Both are accountable. Both are invited into the hard, holy work of reconciliation.

This is not inequality. It is holy empowerment.

Yes, emotional and sexual disappointments can hurt, frustrate, and anger us. We may reach a breaking point and cry out to God, "What's the point?" Paul answers that question with clarity: The point is restoration. Not pretending nothing happened, but moving toward healing rather than walking away.

Reconciliation does not minimize the pain. It dignifies it by insisting it is worth resolving.

Reflection

- How does God's clear call to reconciliation reshape your sense of responsibility in marriage?

- What would it look like to pursue resolution instead of waiting for your spouse to move first?

- How might embracing reconciliation help you reunite around shared purpose rather than past hurt?

- What if disagreement isn't about winning or losing but about two teammates adjusting the plan to move forward together? What change would that make?

- Are you in a season where a third party, who understands the emotional and sexual challenges in marriage, could come alongside you with the S.T.E.P. approach (in the next section) to help you find common ground, rebuild trust, and guide you both toward mutual understanding, healing, and renewed intimacy?

Key Thought

These scriptures don't limit you but liberate you. They show that your differences aren't obstacles to unity but the very path to it. Because they call for humility, love, respect, and patience.

Yes, you're on the same team. Yes, you're aiming for the same summit. But you'll take different paths. That's not a threat. It's the design. Some weeks, you will hike your spouse's trail. Other weeks, your spouse will hike yours.

Because the goal isn't whose path is chosen. The goal is reaching the summit of mutual emotional and sexual satisfaction.

LIGHTBULB MOMENT #6

SAME TEAM, SAME GOAL, DIFFERENT PLAYS

Practical Application

You and your spouse are teammates, not twins. Marriage isn't about sameness. If you are the same, one of you is unnecessary. You are male and female with different preferences. Yet you both need and desire emotional and sexual satisfaction (1 Corinthians 7:1–5). That's why in conflict, you need a neon reminder: "Same Team, Same Goal, Different Plays."

Most conflict isn't right vs. wrong. It's preference vs. preference. This happens throughout the day. For example, one time Sarah and I wanted to visit our daughter in Paris and needed to travel from southern France to do so. I wanted to take the train. She wanted to fly. Same destination. Different routes.

We can argue endlessly about the *how* and miss the fact that we already agree on *where* we're headed.

Why This Changes Everything

Reset phrases like "Same team, same goal, different plays" help couples thrive under pressure because they shift the tone from adversarial to collaborative. There's something powerful when someone declares, "Remember, we're teammates, not opponents!"

- Where could this phrase "same team, same goal, different plays" help you stay grounded?

- How important is it for you to stay focused on the shared goal when differing on the method to achieve that goal?

Although this is a personal study, you and your spouse might like to do the following S.T.E.P. exercise together. I invite you to gently bring it up to them. But if they're not ready or choose to decline, please don't lose heart, as I will also help you follow the acronym S.T.E.P. alone.

S.T.E.P. As a Team: How to Move Forward Together

When preferences clash, especially around emotional and sexual connection, you need more than patience. You need a process. (I need to provide a warning here. If one or both of you are not ready to address the issue of intimacy, then change the topic to something minor like this week's scheduling of family plans, which weekend project to do, or a date-night activity. First experience a small success as you step through S.T.E.P. Later, return to the below topic.)

Often:

- Husbands feel emotionally connected through physical intimacy.
- Wives feel physically open through emotional connection.

Who's right in their feelings? You both are. God didn't make you identical. He made you interdependent (1 Corinthians 11:11).

- Same team: God joined you together.
- Same goal: You both long for closeness.
- Different plays: You start from different places.

Let's S.T.E.P. forward.

State the Issue Clearly

Speak honestly without blame:

> "We both want to feel close, but I want to start on the emotional end, which conflicts with your desire to start on the sexual side of things."
>
> "Yes, I agree, we both want to feel close, but as you said, I prefer to begin with sexual intimacy and then talk as we lie there in bed."

Talk About Your Perspective

Own your wiring:

> "For me, emotional closeness leads to physical openness. I want sexual intimacy, but not when that is an end in itself. Otherwise, if that is all there is, I feel used. I don't say that to dishonor you but to convey what arouses me sexually, and that is when I feel loved for who I am apart from sex."
>
> "For me, physical closeness leads to emotional connection. I can feel this build up sexually and need that release in order to feel bonded to you. I get it that you can

feel used, and I feel badly about that, but I see it as having a need only you can meet. Then, when we're close physically, I feel reassured and wanted. That, in turn, opens me up emotionally."

Remember that this is about mutual understanding, not proving who's right.

Evaluate the Shared Vision
Both of you here say:

"God intended for us to be one in the bedroom. He created us male and female, both needing emotional and sexual satisfaction. But we often start at different ends of the spectrum. God does not intend for one of us to win and the other to lose. He intends for us to find a win-win, where both experience emotional and sexual fulfillment. We may arrive at that satisfaction through different pathways, but we can find common ground—like talking heart-to-heart without a sexual agenda and also enjoying sex itself as a way to meet a real physical need that profoundly impacts our emotional and spiritual health [1 Corinthians 7:5]."

Plan Forward (Make It Doable Emotionally *and* Sexually)
You've acknowledged your differences. You've talked about your shared goal. Now it's time to make a practical, low-pressure plan—one that includes *both* emotional and sexual connection.

Use the 5 Ws + H as a guide, not to fix everything, but to take a next step *together*.

- **Who** will take the next step emotionally or sexually?

  "I want to offer you my full attention three times a week for the next six weeks, no strings attached, just to hear your heart and show you I'm truly with you."

  "I will prepare and take the initiative for our sexual intimacy once a week for the next six weeks to meet a need you have that only I can meet."

- **What** might make this difficult to do given what is in front of us over the next six weeks?

  "I am out of town for four days next week."

- **When** and **Where** is the best time and place for this connection, without stress or exhaustion?

  "Let's meet next Tuesday at 6:00 p.m. at the dining room table."

- **Why** is this important?

  "We need each other, as 1 Corinthians 7:1–5 reveals."

- **How** can we let the other know of our appreciation?

  "Thanks for talking to me each of those three evenings for fifteen minutes. That meant so much to me."

  "Thanks for initiating our love-making. Wow. Thank you for caring."

S.T.E.P. When You're Alone in the Process

State the Issue Clearly (from both sides)

Begin by honestly identifying the issue not just from your perspective but also from your spouse's. Do this not from what you think but by truly getting in tune with what they think (right or wrong in the moment).

> "From your vantage point, I think you may feel I am . . ." [e.g., controlling, dismissive, unloving, disrespectful].
>
> "From my view, I have a need that only you can meet, which I hope you see as a compliment, not a complaint because . . ." [e.g., I feel lonely, misunderstood, sexually disconnected].

This dual-awareness helps you avoid defensiveness and remain grounded in humility.

Talk About Their Perspective with Empathy

Even if your spouse isn't ready to engage, practice seeing the world through their eyes.

> Acknowledge their likely concerns, emotions, and hesitations: "As tough as it is for me to confess this, I can see those moments when I have appeared controlling, dismissive, unloving, and disrespectful."

When the opportunity comes, invite them into the conversation—not to argue your side but to share ideas with a posture of, "I might not be right, and you're not wrong. Can we explore this together?"

Evaluate the Shared Vision

Despite your differences, remember what you agree on. You're still on the same team, pursuing the same core goals: shared love and respect, effectiveness in parenting, unity in finances, trust and passion in intimacy. Reminding yourself of the common ground you have with your spouse will help reset the tone toward unity, not rivalry.

Plan Forward (with the 5 Ws + H)

Use this as a quiet reflection exercise to help you move toward your spouse with humility and intentionality. Remember, you're not planning *for* them—you're planning *toward* them.

- **Who** do they need you to be in this moment?
- **What** could make emotional or sexual connection easier for them?
- **When** are they most open or at ease?
- **Where** do they tend to feel most relaxed and connected?
- **Why** is this connection important—not just for you, but for them?
- **How** might you invite them into a step forward without pressure?

This exercise isn't about crafting the perfect moment. It's about building understanding and creating space for trust. Think of it as preparing the ground—not forcing growth but making connection possible.

Closing Thought

The more you seek to understand your spouse's sentiment and the way they see the situation, the more you create space for them to feel safe, valued, and willing to engage. For both of you, you don't have to have all the answers. You just need to remember who you're fighting for, not who you're fighting with. Same team. Same goal.

Weekly Check-In

Sometime this week, after both you and your spouse have completed the personal studies, take fifteen minutes to meet together and reflect on your key takeaways. *Remember, this is not a time for you to complain, accuse, or blame each other but a time for you to come together and share how God encouraged you with this content.* Use the following prompts to get the conversation started.

Suggested Questions [PICK 2 TO 3]

- As you reflect on this session, what lightbulb moment blessed you the most?
- What encouraged you most about the difference between simply communicating and truly understanding each other?
- What encouraged you about both of you being on the same team with the same goals from the Lord's vantage point, even if your approaches are sometimes different?
- What part of the five-step "whiteboard" exercise resonated most with you about what the two of you do well together in your conversations?
- Looking back at the S.T.E.P. exercise, what stood out to you the most as something the two of you already do well when working toward a decision?

Looking Ahead

Read **chapters 7–8** in *Lightbulb Moments in Marriage* before the next group gathering. Use the space below to note anything that stands out, challenges you, or encourages you.

BEFORE GROUP MEETING	Read chapters 7–8 in *Lightbulb Moments in Marriage* Read the Welcome section (page 82)
GROUP MEETING	Discuss the Connect questions (pages 82–83) Watch the video teaching for session 4 and take notes (pages 83–86) Engage in a Group Discussion on the material (pages 86–88) Couples have a Husband and Wife Discussion (page 88) Close in Group Prayer (page 88)
PERSONAL STUDY	
LIGHTBULB MOMENT #7: BIBLICAL FOUNDATION	Complete the Biblical Foundation personal study for Lightbulb Moment #7 (pages 90–92)
LIGHTBULB MOMENT #7: PRACTICAL APPLICATION	Complete the Practical Application personal study for Lightbulb Moment #7 (pages 93–95)
LIGHTBULB MOMENT #8: BIBLICAL FOUNDATION	Complete the Biblical Foundation personal study for Lightbulb Moment #8 (pages 96–98)
LIGHTBULB MOMENT #8: PRACTICAL APPLICATION	Complete the Practical Application personal study for Lightbulb Moment #8 (pages 99–102)
WEEKLY CHECK-IN	Connect with your spouse during the week to discuss your key insights from this session (page 103)
BEFORE NEXT WEEK	Read chapters 9–10 in *Lightbulb Moments in Marriage*

SESSION FOUR

OUR ACKNOWLEDGMENT AND OUR TENSION

LIGHTBULB #7:

Not Wrong, Just Different Shades of Right

Marriage thrives when differing preferences and perspectives are acknowledged as valid in the gray areas—different shades of right.

LIGHTBULB #8:

Don't Let the 20% Define the 80%

Frustrations and shortcomings are real, but goodwill and front-side strengths often offset backside weaknesses.

Welcome [READ ON YOUR OWN]

Welcome to session four. By now, you've likely had a few *aha* and *uh-oh* moments. That's normal. Growth in marriage often comes through friction. As Proverbs 27:17 reminds us, "As iron sharpens iron, so one person sharpens another."

Here are two lightbulb moments that can change how couples grow.

Lightbulb Moment #7 focuses on your *acknowledgment* in marriage. You recognize that neither you nor your spouse is wrong, just different shades of right. You and your spouse may approach things like laundry, parenting, or storytelling in very different ways. That doesn't make either of you wrong. Often, it's simply a matter of preference. In our home, Sarah and I joke, "That's less better," and I'll say, "Mine's more better." It's our way of keeping things light and honoring our differences without judgment.

Lightbulb Moment #8 addresses the *tension* in marriage and, specifically, to not allowing the 20% to define the 80%. Every marriage includes about 20% tension—personality quirks, recurring frustrations, or misfires. The problem is when that small percentage is allowed to overshadow the 80% that is good, faithful, and worth celebrating. God doesn't ask us to ignore the 20%, but He does ask us to focus first on what is true, honorable, lovely, and commendable (Philippians 4:8).

This week, choose to see your spouse through that lens. Not through a single frustrating moment but through the faithful life you are building together. Your marriage is not defined by what is hard unless you let it be. So enter this session with open hands. Let go of judgment and the need to be right. Marriage is not a courtroom. It is a sanctuary, a place to grow in grace.

Let the lightbulbs turn on.

Connect [5 TO 15 MINUTES]

Get the session started by choosing one or all of the following questions to discuss:

- Can you think of a moment recently when you realized, "We definitely see this differently," and simply allowed there to be a difference without turning it into a conflict? (Example: Sarah now accepts that I don't like pepper on my eggs. Early in our marriage, she'd say, "Eggs are no good without pepper," and add it anyway. Now we just smile at the difference.)

— *or* —

- Is there something about your spouse that used to frustrate you but now you see as a strength? (Example: Sarah's desire for a clean, organized home used to feel like pressure to clean up my office, but now I see it as a reminder that she cares, and I'm grateful.)

— *or* —

- When life gets busy, what helps you step back and notice what's steady and good in your relationship? (Example: One message I often share is to assume goodwill in your spouse. We'll sometimes say, "We both have goodwill here, even if we don't like each other right now." And that's enough to get us through the moment.)

Watch [30 TO 40 MINUTES]

As you begin today's session, ask God to give you fresh eyes not just to see your marriage more clearly but also to notice how He's using it to grow you in gratitude, grace, and connection. As you watch, jot down any thoughts that speak to your heart. Many key ideas are already outlined here so you can stay fully present.

Outline: Lightbulb Moments #7 & #8

I. Lightbulb Moment #7—Our Acknowledgment: Not Wrong, Just Different Shades of Right

- The Core Insight
    - We instinctively think: If I'm right, my spouse must be wrong.
    - But many conflicts are not about right or wrong. They're preferences, not moral failings.
    - We need a way to say: "Not wrong, just different."
- Common Examples
    - Milk Carton: Which shelf is "right"? Neither. It's preference.
    - Parenting Times: Discipline vs. rest. Both value the child.
    - Dishwasher: Trying to help, not wrong.
    - Storytelling: Elaborating versus getting to the point.
- Biblical Lens—Romans 14
    - Disputable matters existed even in the early church (eat meat or not? Friday night Sabbath or Sunday?).
    - Paul: "Stop judging your brother with contempt."
    - "Who are you to judge another's servant?"
- Marriage Application
    - Just like early believers, spouses differ on convictions and preferences.
    - The solution isn't "winning" the argument but mutual respect in the gray zones.
- Sarah and I Sometimes . . .
    - Use the phrase "less better" as a humorous way to acknowledge differences.

- Reassure each other with: "You're not wrong." I will add, "Sarah, Jesus listens to you more than He listens to me.")

Five Practical Tools:

1. Name the gray zone: "This isn't sin, just preference."
2. Replace judgment with curiosity: "Can you help me understand why this matters to you?"
3. Use healthy phrases: "We both want what's good and right."
4. Validate before you debate: "I can tell this matters to you."
5. Drop the gavel: "I'm not your judge in the gray zones."

Stories and Breakthroughs:

- A wife saw her husband as lazy, but it was a difference in parenting style.
- A husband judged his wife's hospitality but learned it was how she came alive.
- Dishwasher legacy: The tension melted after the wife learned it came from his dad.
- A husband's Friday night compromise: "Her people, my peace."

II. Lightbulb Moment #8—Our Tension: Don't Let the 20% Define the 80%

- The 80/20 Marriage Insight:
  - Every marriage has about 20% tension.
  - Don't let that 20% become the whole story.
  - What we focus on grows.
- Attraction Turns to Irritation:
  - Couples often *attract* and then attack over the same trait.
  - Front-side strength becomes back-side weakness.
- Biblical Realism—1 Corinthians 7:28
  - "Those who marry will face many troubles in this life."
  - Marriage includes joy and difficulty. That's normal, not failure.

Common "Sandpaper" Differences:

- Withdraw vs. process
- Planner vs. spontaneous
- Structure vs. spontaneity

- Underneath the Differences:
  - Spiritual gifts: mercy vs. exhortation
  - Upbringing, gender, personality

- The Snapshot vs. Movie Principle:
  - Don't take a bad moment (snapshot) and let it define your marriage (movie).
  - Even Sarah and I have heated moments, but we don't build a case from them.
- Goodwill as the Assumption:
  - "Unless you married Hitler's cousin . . ." Most spouses have goodwill, not malice.
  - Ask, "Is this flaw from sin or just human limitation?"
- Shifting Perspective:
  - *Women*: listing positives often restores affection.
  - *Men*: see that wife's concern often comes from care, not contempt.
- Final Challenge:
  - Don't judge a Peter as if he's a Judas.
  - Frustration is real, but let your belief in goodwill be greater.
  - Gratitude restores the big picture.
  - Don't wait until they're gone to realize what you had.

Takeaway Testimonies:

- "I stopped judging and started listening. We became a team."
- "Her people, my peace" became a slogan for compromise and unity.
- "Remember, I'm good-willed, and so are you."

Notes

Use this space to jot down what moved you, challenged you, or gave you fresh perspective.

Notes

Group Discussion [30 TO 45 MINUTES]

As we begin, remember this is a space for encouragement. No one has all the answers, but each of us brings something valuable: our story, our perspective, and our desire to walk more closely with Christ. Let's invite God into this time and trust Him to strengthen our hearts, deepen our understanding, and draw us closer, to Him and to one another.

You won't cover everything here, and that's okay. Read through it, and if something stands out, pause and ask, "Why this?" That moment might be your lightbulb moment.

Many marital tensions aren't about sin but about differences in wiring, personality, or style. But when we assume, *"I'm right, so you must be wrong,"* we move from disagreement to judgment. However, seeing the "gray zones" can shift everything.

Group Reflection Prompts

1. Think of a recent disagreement that was really about different styles—not right or wrong. How would calling it a "gray zone" have changed the tone? Sarah and I sometimes say, "That's less better" to keep it light in tense moments. Have you had a "less better" moment lately? Could humor have helped?
2. Read Romans 14:1–4. Paul acknowledges the reality of "disputable matters." How might this guide how you speak to your spouse when you differ?
3. Next time you feel strongly about something, what might happen if you started with, "Help me understand why this matters to you"?
4. I've said, "You can be right but wrong at the top of your voice." What helps you stay respectful when emotions run high?
5. What speaks to you from this poem?

You said pink, I saw blue
We both thought the other never knew
Not wrong, just different shades of right.

Aha! A lightbulb burns so bright
We're not broken, we must reframe.
With love and respect, we can change.

6. Every marriage has about 20% of ongoing tension—small differences or annoyances. But that doesn't mean the marriage is broken. The danger is letting that 20% eclipse the 80% that's good, faithful, and beautiful. Which of these "different shades of right" have you welcomed into your marriage?

    - Withdraw vs. Process: *One needs space to think; the other needs to talk it out.*
    - Planner vs. Spontaneous: *One finds peace in preparation; the other finds life in flexibility.*
    - Structure vs. Fluidity: *One thrives with routine; the other flows with what the day brings.*
    - Detail-Oriented vs. Big Picture Thinker: *One sees what's missing; the other sees where it's going.*
    - Direct vs. Diplomatic: *One says what they mean; the other says it subtly.*
    - Emotion-First vs. Logic-First: *One starts with how it feels; the other starts with what makes sense.*

7. How has focusing on your "80%" helped you respond with more gratitude? What habits—like prayer, humor, or remembering shared goals—help you see your spouse in a more balanced light?
8. How does assuming your spouse has goodwill change the way you approach conflict? What happens when you believe they're not trying to hurt you but are just reacting from stress or need?
9. First Corinthians 7:33–34 reminds us that a husband or wife wants to please their spouse. Why is it important to believe your spouse isn't trying to frustrate you but truly wants to do the caring thing, or at least isn't trying to displease you?
10. "*Unless you married Hitler's cousin.*" Why does assuming goodwill help in hard moments?
11. Some people take a snapshot of their spouse in a bad moment and let that image define the relationship. What would it look like to view the whole movie of your marriage—not just a difficult scene?

Real-Life Reminder:

- "I used to focus on the 20% he didn't do—but now I see the 80% he brings every day."
- "We're both goodwilled—we're just different."
- "That realization brought us closer than any date night ever had."

As you close, remember that you don't have to agree on everything. The goal is deeper understanding. You're learning to blend strengths and appreciate the different ways each processes life. Keep going, a step at a time. It's worth every step.

Husband and Wife Discussion [5 TO 15 MINUTES]

Keep in mind this is a sacred space to share what's touching your heart. Use phrases like:

- "This helped me see . . ."
- "Something I'm grateful for is . . ."
- "I was encouraged by . . ."
- "This made me want to grow in . . ."

Let this be a moment of gentle, personal reflection. Once again, you don't need to use every prompt—just let one open the door to deeper connection.

Conversation Starters

1. "I appreciated something someone shared during group time."
   It helped me see ________________. It reminded me I'm not alone in ________________.
2. "This line really spoke to me . . ."
   "Not wrong, just different shades of right." That helps me stay grounded when we see things differently.
3. "I'm grateful for this reminder from God's Word . . ."
   That goodwill is key to a healthy marriage. That our differences are part of God's design—not defects.
4. "The 80/20 idea impacted me . . ."
   It helped me not let a small moment define the big picture. I want to focus more on what's strong and good between us.
5. "Something I want to carry forward from this week is . . ."
   A spirit of grace in our differences. Trusting that we're for each other—even when we disagree.

Group Prayer [5 TO 10 MINUTES]

Close in silence or prayer. One of you may say, *"Lord, thank You for speaking to our hearts. Thank You for reminding us we're not enemies—we're teammates. Help us remember the 80%, the goodwill, and the grace You give us daily. In Your strength, help us live that out together. Amen."*

SESSION FOUR

PERSONAL STUDY

During this week's group time, you explored how much of life plays out in the gray areas. The way forward isn't always black and white, just different shades of right. You also discussed how your spouse, like you, will fall short at times, but you don't have to let the 20% that's hard overshadow the 80% that's good. These truths, and more, are what you'll reflect on in God's Word this week. Before you begin, ask the Lord to open your heart to what He wants to show you and how it applies to your marriage. Keep writing down your thoughts to share with your spouse later. If you're reading *Lightbulb Moments in Marriage* alongside this study, begin with chapters 7–8.

LIGHTBULB MOMENT #7

NOT WRONG, JUST DIFFERENT SHADES OF RIGHT

Biblical Foundation

How does God call us to navigate gray-area differences, especially when we feel deeply confident that we're right in what we think, feel, or believe, and yet someone else sees it differently? Welcome to Romans 14. This is a chapter where Paul addresses:

- our attitude toward those who see things differently;
- the assumptions we carry into disagreements;
- our tendency to elevate preferences into moral high ground; and
- our instinct to divide over non-essential differences.

This was written to a divided church. Though these folks wished to honor God, they also judged each other with contempt along the way.

In first-century Rome, believers clashed over food, festivals, and traditions. These weren't moral issues but gray areas. Yet instead of walking in grace, they slipped into judgment and contempt. So, Paul steps in, not to settle the debate, but to call them to something higher:

- A faith big enough to hold differing convictions
- A love and respect strong enough to resist superiority
- A community humble enough to make allowances in the gray

Your marriage may have more in common with the Roman church than you realize. If you've ever disagreed over parenting styles, chore routines, worship preferences, or how to spend a Saturday, you're already living in Romans 14 territory.

Now picture this: a Jewish believer and a Gentile believer, married in Christ, trying to live as one. One celebrates dietary laws and Sabbath traditions. The other feels complete freedom in Christ. Both love God. Both have convictions. But the tension? Very real.

Romans 14 wasn't written for people arguing over sin but for people divided over sincere convictions. And that's where many couples find themselves today.

So let's dig into the tensions of the early church. Get ready to learn that sometimes, being "right" isn't the goal.

Romans 14:1–4

"Accept the one whose faith is weak, without quarreling over disputable matters. One person's faith allows them to eat anything, but another, whose faith is weak, eats only vegetables. The one who eats everything must not treat with contempt the one who does not, and the one who does not eat everything must not judge the one who does, for God has accepted them. Who are you to judge someone else's servant? To their own master, servants stand or fall. And they will stand, for the Lord is able to make them stand."

Romans 14:10

"You, then, why do you judge your brother or sister? Or why do you treat them with contempt?"

Romans 14:13

"Therefore let us stop passing judgment on one another. Instead, make up your mind not to put any stumbling block or obstacle in the way of a brother or sister."

Romans 14:19

"Let us therefore make every effort to do what leads to peace and to mutual edification."

The Roman church was a cultural mix.

- Jewish Christians still honored Mosaic traditions by avoiding certain foods and observing sacred days.
- Gentile Christians felt no obligation to those customs.

Both wanted to honor God, but they reached different conclusions. The problem wasn't rebellion; it was conviction. But instead of respect, judgment and contempt took over. Paul, himself a Jew, didn't settle the debate. Instead, he said:

- Don't quarrel over disputable matters (verse 1).
- Stop judging (verse 13).
- Pursue peace (verse 19).

His message:

- Each believer answers to God.
- Unity matters more than uniformity.
- Gracious allowance in the gray areas is a mark of spiritual maturity.

This isn't relativism. Paul isn't saying all views are equally right. But he is revealing that we must allow for a spectrum of rightness. Our phrase for this lightbulb moment must be applied: "Not Wrong, Just Different Shades of Right."

The Roman church was split not by sin but by sincere convictions. Paul refused to take sides. Instead, he pointed both groups to a higher standard: humble acceptance and peace. The result is a timeless teaching on how to navigate gray areas. We must resist saying, "You're wrong for thinking that way" and "You're less than me because of it." We must not moralize and assume our way is the only way.

Summary

- Not all differences are sinful: many are just cultural, temperamental, or personal.
- You are not the other's judge: God is.
- Contempt is lethal: it kills connection and fosters pride.
- Grace leads to peace, but peace requires effort.
- Unity is not sameness: it's honoring the other, even when you disagree.

Reflection

♦ Where is God inviting you to accept someone with a different conviction, without trying to change them (Romans 14:1)?

♦ Where might you be judging someone with contempt instead of acknowledging their different shade of right (Romans 14:13)?

♦ What's one practical way you can pursue peace and mutual upbuilding in this situation (Romans 14:19)?

Try New Language This Week:

- "This isn't wrong, it's just different."
- "Help me understand your view instead of trying to fix it."
- "Let's agree that this is a preference, not an absolute."
- "God has accepted you. I want to accept you too."

Let This Sink In:

Paul wasn't just stopping a food fight. He was redefining spiritual maturity. We tend to think maturity means stronger convictions. But Romans 14 teaches this: It's not just what you believe; it's how you treat those who believe differently in the gray areas.

NOT WRONG, JUST DIFFERENT SHADES OF RIGHT

Practical Application

"You can be right but wrong at the top of your voice."

I've said this many times, because I've lived it. Most marital conflict isn't about sin; it's about differences. Backgrounds, personalities, convictions, and styles aren't right or wrong, they're just different. And when we stop moralizing those differences—that is, when we name them as "gray zones"—grace enters the room.

Here are five practices that help move us from judgment to connection.

1. Name the Gray Zone

Not everything is black and white. Naming a disagreement as a "gray zone" disarms the argument and makes room for sincerity—even when you see things differently. It's not about brushing things off with, "No big deal, just a gray zone." This is about acceptance, not dismissiveness. Naming it opens the heart, not shuts down the conversation. Sarah and I use the phrase, "That's less better." It makes us laugh and reminds us this isn't sin, it's just a shade of right. It's not polished, but it reminds us we're not enemies, we just see things differently.

Pause and reflect: Was there a recent moment where naming a gray zone could have helped?

2. Replace Judgment with Curiosity

Instead of correcting, try understanding. Ask: *"Can you help me understand why this matters to you?"* That question has defused countless tensions in our marriage. One woman told me she used to criticize how her husband loaded the dishwasher, until she learned it was how his dad taught him. Besides, he was loading the dishwasher!

3. Use Honoring Language

Words matter in tension. Some helpful phrases:

- "It sounds like we both want what's good."
- "You're not wrong. I just see it differently."
- "Help me understand what's important to you here."

Saying "You're not wrong" isn't saying you are wrong but valuing your spouse's opinion.

4. Validate Before You Debate

You can't argue your way into closeness. But you can listen your way there. A husband once said to his wife, *"I can tell this matters deeply to you. I want to understand why."* That sentence turned a debate into a dialogue. **Try this:** "Remember, even though we don't agree, you matter more to me than my point does."

5. Drop the Gavel

You are not your spouse's judge. One wife said, "I realized I wasn't correcting. I was judging. I dropped the gavel, and we became allies again." Ask yourself: "Am I acting like the judge, or like a teammate?" When you demand control for "peace of mind," you might be sacrificing peace between you.

Private Reflection

- Do you consider your spouse's opinion when it differs from yours? On a scale of 1–10, rate it.

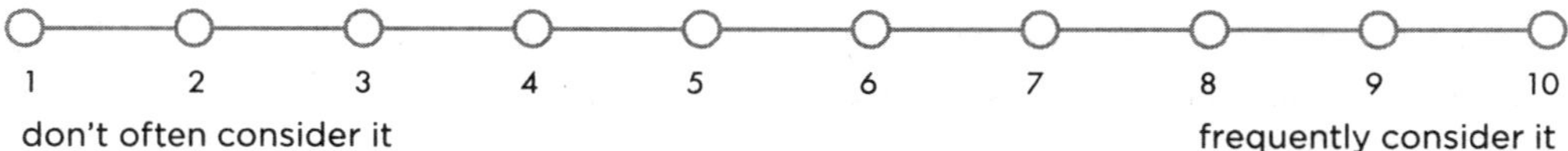

If you gave a rating of 6 or higher, did you honestly consider your spouse's view because you acknowledge "neither of us is wrong, we just see different shades of right"?

- Think of a recent disagreement. Did you . . .

    - Turn preference into a moral issue?
    - Assume bad motives?
    - Act like judge and jury?
    - Push instead of pause?
    - Though "more" right, did you end up being wrong because you shouted at your spouse at the top of your voice?

What do your answers reveal? What can you confess or change?

- ♦ Are you prone to **confirmation bias**—you only notice what supports your view? (Try asking, "What have I seen lately that supports their perspective?")

- ♦ Are you prone to **assumption bias**—you already decided why they did it? (Instead, ask, "Could there be a good reason I've overlooked?")

- ♦ Are you prone to **moral superiority bias**—you assume your way is more spiritual? (Ask, "Has my tone been more condemning than constructive?")

Closing Thought

So this week . . .

- Drop the gavel.
- Laugh a little more.
- Listen a little longer.
- Honor the gray zones.

Let the lightbulb come on: "Wow . . . this is so true. I need to acknowledge this. Neither of us is wrong, we just see different shades of right."

LIGHTBULB MOMENT #8

DON'T LET THE 20% DEFINE THE 80%

Biblical Foundation

If there's one thing I wish couples better understood, it's this: *Tension in marriage isn't always a sign of failure but can be a sign of normalcy.* Friction doesn't mean something's broken. It means you're married. God's Word doesn't just explain this; it validates it.

Let's look at four passages that frame the 20% tension all couples face. These will help us see it through a biblical lens.

1 Corinthians 7:28

"But those who marry will face many troubles in this life, and I want to spare you this."

Paul reminds the Corinthian believers that marriage brings "trouble," from the Greek word *thlipsis,* meaning pressure, distress, or hardship. Paul is not trying to scare them but to prepare them. Marriage offers deep intimacy, but it also brings tension. One of the clearest areas we see that tension is in the bedroom. Might we say that is part of the 20%?

Just a few verses earlier, Paul gives another surprising and profound insight.

1 Corinthians 7:4

"The wife does not have authority over her own body but yields it to her husband. In the same way, the husband does not have authority over his own body but yields it to his wife."

This mutual yielding was revolutionary in Paul's time (and still is today). No other human institution operates this way. In marriage, both the husband and wife are given final say over one another's body. That is not a formula for ease. It's part of the 20%—a setup for struggle, surrender, and spiritual growth.

The "trouble" Paul refers to includes this very dynamic. Shared authority in the most intimate space requires humility, sacrifice, and grace. It invites a kind of yielding that is unfamiliar in most areas of life. And yet, it is by God's design.

When a husband and wife get it right in the most private space, they often get it right in the public ones too. Not because every problem disappears but because the core of their marriage is rooted in mutual surrender, just as Ephesians 5:21 teaches: "Submit to one another out of reverence for Christ." Instead of each asserting their authority, each yields to the other's, not out of weakness, but out of worship.

That's where peace grows. That's where oneness thrives.

1 Corinthians 7:33–34

"But a married man is concerned about . . . how he can please his wife. . . . A married woman is concerned about . . . how she can please her husband."

Paul here contrasts the focus of single and married believers, but he assumes something powerful: In marriage, both spouses want to please each other. The Greek word *areskō* ("to please") shows a heart of thoughtful concern. Even when imperfect, most spouses are trying. That's the 80% we're called to notice and honor.

But when we face the 20% consisting of disappointments and differences, it's easy to forget that intent. We start assuming the worst: *They don't care. They're doing this on purpose.* After all, we told them of our frustration and they did it again!

It is here that Paul invites us to see goodwill, not indifference or ill-will.

Matthew 26:41

"Watch and pray so that you will not fall into temptation. The spirit is willing, but the flesh is weak."

Jesus says this to His sleepy disciples in Gethsemane, not to condemn them but to acknowledge their hearts were in the right place, even if their actions failed. We can do the same in marriage. Much of what frustrates us isn't carnal rebellion; it's human limitation or weakness.

It is goodwill without good follow through. Fatigue happens. Forgetfulness happens. Stress happens. Weakness of the flesh happens.

What if we followed Jesus' lead and said, "I see your willing spirit"? That kind of grace would change how we interpret each other's flaws and re-center us on love and respect (Ephesians 5:33).

Marriage brings God-designed tension, especially where two people must share authority, like in the bedroom. But this isn't dysfunction; it's opportunity. Scripture teaches us to assume goodwill, embrace mutual surrender, and extend grace in the face of weakness.

Reflection

- When Paul says "those who marry will face many troubles" (1 Corinthians 7:28), do you see that as failure or part of the fallen world we live in and that which God uses to refine us—as troubling as trouble is?

- In what areas might our "trouble" be a divine opportunity to grow in Christlike love, respect, and trust?

- How does mutual authority (1 Corinthians 7:4) challenge the way you think about control and yielding in the bedroom? Where might you need to trust more and control less considering shared authority in the bedroom?

- Do you sometimes moralize personality differences as spiritual failures in your spouse, or even in yourself?

- Paul assumes spouses want to please each other. How does that change how you interpret your spouse's less-than-better tone or choices?

- Are you more focused on where your spouse falls short or where they're trying? Do you have a restricted standard about how they should try, and when they fall short there, you judge and condemn?

- Do Jesus' words, "The spirit is willing, but the flesh is weak" (Matthew 26:41) help you offer more compassion to your spouse? (Remember, Jesus needed Peter, James, and John in the garden of Gethsemane, and they failed Him. But still, He looked more deeply into their desires to do what was right, and told them so.)

- Have you ignored a willing spirit in your spouse because you were too focused on their weak actions that failed you in your time of need?

- How would your view of conflict change if you saw some of it as divinely designed for you to see the 80% and not just the 20%?

LIGHTBULB MOMENT #8

DON'T LET THE 20% DEFINE THE 80%

Practical Application

Every marriage has its share of tension—the 20% where your differences grate, frustrate, or confuse you. But that 20% doesn't cancel out the 80% of goodwill and common goals that brought you and your spouse together in the first place. What defines your marriage isn't the snapshot of a hard moment but the full movie of God's work through your story of two people He joined together.

Let me confess: Sarah and I have had plenty of tense moments. But we've learned to spot the signs: tone, sarcasm, short replies, faulty assumptions. Instead of judging each other, we hit pause. We call timeout. We reset. One moment of friction doesn't become the whole story.

If someone snapped a photo of us at our worst, it wouldn't tell the truth about our marriage. That's the point. Unless the moment involves serious harm, it's just a human moment, not a moral failure. Maybe, for example, it's the silent treatment that lasted longer than it should have. That's not evidence of a broken marriage; it's a snapshot of two imperfect people trying to figure things out.

Perspective, not perfection, keeps us grounded. We know the difference between a rough moment and a wrecked marriage. So we remind each other of our goodwill and that we are teammates.

Here's the challenge:

- Don't fixate on flaws.
- Don't weaponize weakness.
- Don't let a snapshot replace the full story.

Step back and you'll often see that your spouse isn't trying to hurt you. They're human. They're probably reacting from a place of feeling unloved or disrespected. That's not something to criticize but something to comprehend. They are reacting to what they feel is an unmet need, not trying to neglect yours.

Reflect and Reset: Ten Questions for Seeing the 80%

1. What does your spouse do well that you've been overlooking?
(*Write it down. Thank God for it. Tell them.*)

2. When did you last catch your spouse doing something "right"?
   (*Let that moment reshape your view.*)
3. What front-side strength of your spouse has a back-side weakness?
   (*For example, their attention to detail may feel like micromanaging, but it comes from a desire to serve with excellence.*)
4. Has the 20% hijacked your attitude lately?
   (*If so, what part of the 80% can you refocus on?*)
5. Are you holding a "snapshot" of your spouse in a negative light?
   (*If so, could the whole movie show faithfulness you've forgotten?*)
6. How would your tone change if you believed your spouse really did want to please you, even if imperfectly?
   (*For example, you might say, "Thank you for trying. I see the effort."*)
7. How would you finish this sentence: "When I think about who my spouse is at their core, I'm grateful that they . . ."
   (*For example, "I'm grateful that they work so hard for our family."*)
8. Has one frustration overshadowed your spouse's ongoing faithfulness?
   (*For example, your spouse may not initiate conversation, but they always respond with their presence when you do.*)
9. How has your spouse grown since you met?
   (*Name two or three areas of maturity or transformation.*)
10. How can you encourage a front-side strength in your spouse despite its weakness?
    (*For example, you could say, "I value your conviction," even if it sometimes comes across to you as stubbornness.*)

Score Yourself

Score yourself based on your answers to these ten questions. How often do you focus on your spouse's 20% (non-sinful flaws)?

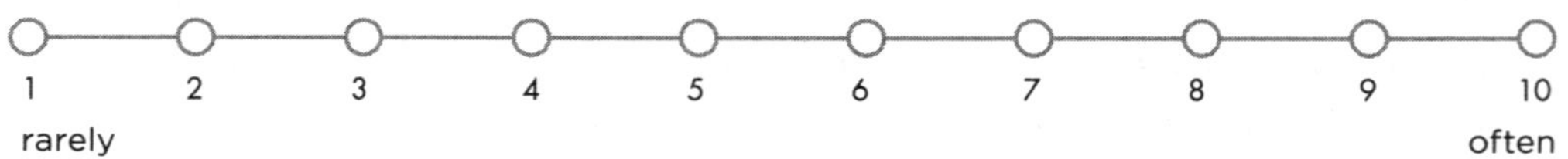

♦ If you circled 6 or above, when did you last react in anger over something that wasn't sin in your spouse but was just a difference?

Appreciate vs. Annoy

In the following chart, list eight traits you appreciate about your spouse on the left. Then list two traits that annoy you on the right.

Traits You Appreciate	Traits That Annoy You
1.	1.
2.	2.
3.	
4.	
5.	
6.	
7.	
8.	

- Now ask yourself, *Which strengths first attracted you? Which have you lost sight of?*

Remember the Real Battle

Peter said, "Your enemy the devil prowls around like a roaring lion looking for someone to devour" (1 Peter 5:8).

- Is the enemy trying to divide you and your spouse through difference?

- What's one way you can fight back with love and respect?

Five Lenses to See Your Spouse Differently

1. **See the real enemy.**
   Is the enemy trying to divide you (1 Corinthians 7:5; Ephesians 4:26–27)?
2. **See what Jesus sees.**
   Could a weakness or wound be behind their reaction?
3. **See your own sin.**
   Are you reacting with sarcasm or withdrawal?
4. **See your overreaction.**
   Is this issue really about you needing control?
5. **See their need.**
   What longing might be underneath their frustration?

Here's the truth: When you stop fixating on the 20%, you start seeing the whole person again. When you honor the 80%, your marriage shifts from being a battlefield to sacred ground.

Let's not define each other by a hard moment. Let's define each other by daily grace, quiet acts of love and respect, and a lifelong commitment to choosing each other again and again. Your spouse is not trying to fail you. They're just human, just like you. And God is not done with either of you yet (Philippians 1:6).

Weekly Check-In

Sometime this week, after you and your spouse have both completed the personal studies, take about fifteen minutes to meet and reflect on your key takeaways. Use this time to share what encouraged you most.

Suggested Conversation Starters [PICK 2 TO 3]

What really encouraged me this week was . . .

- "I felt challenged, in a good way, to see our differences as gifts, not problems."
- "I noticed that when I paused instead of reacted, our tone softened, and I want more of that."
- "One line from the session stayed with me: _______. I keep thinking about it."
- "This week helped me name something in myself, not in you, that I want to surrender to the Lord."
- "I was encouraged remembering how far we've come since the early days."
- "I'm seeing the goodwill between us, even when things aren't perfect, and that gives me hope."
- "I felt reminded that we're on the same team, even in disagreements, and that brought peace."
- "One moment made me smile. I saw how we're laughing again, even in the messiness."
- "I noticed something you consistently do well, and I'm truly grateful."
- "I felt a quiet peace realizing our differences don't have to divide us. God uses them to shape us."

Looking Ahead

Before the next group gathering, read **chapters 9–10** in *Lightbulb Moments in Marriage.* Use the space below to jot down anything that stands out, challenges you, or encourages you.

BEFORE GROUP MEETING	Read chapters 9–10 in *Lightbulb Moments in Marriage* Read the Welcome section (page 106)
GROUP MEETING	Discuss the Connect questions (page 106) Watch the video teaching for session 5 and take notes (pages 106–110) Engage in a Group Discussion on the material (page 111) Couples have a Husband and Wife Discussion (page 112) Close in Group Prayer (page 112)
PERSONAL STUDY	
LIGHTBULB MOMENT #9: BIBLICAL FOUNDATION	Complete the Biblical Foundation personal study for Lightbulb Moment #9 (pages 114–116)
LIGHTBULB MOMENT #9: PRACTICAL APPLICATION	Complete the Practical Application personal study for Lightbulb Moment #9 (pages 117–119)
LIGHTBULB MOMENT #10: BIBLICAL FOUNDATION	Complete the Biblical Foundation personal study for Lightbulb Moment #10 (pages 120–122)
LIGHTBULB MOMENT #10: PRACTICAL APPLICATION	Complete the Practical Application personal study for Lightbulb Moment #10 (pages 123–124)
WEEKLY CHECK-IN	Connect with your spouse during the week to discuss your key insights from this session (page 125)
BEFORE NEXT WEEK	Read chapters 11–12 in *Lightbulb Moments in Marriage*

SESSION FIVE

OUR SELF-AWARENESS AND OUR AUTHENTICITY

LIGHTBULB #9:

When I Get Defensive, Do I Get Offensive Too?

We often hurt others most when we're protecting ourselves—our shield becomes a club.

LIGHTBULB #10:

Motivation Without Manipulation

Long-lasting influence happens where love and respect are present. The key to motivation is meeting another's deepest need.

Welcome [READ ON YOUR OWN]

In marriage, most of us don't set out to hurt each other—we're usually just trying to protect ourselves. But in the process, our defense can turn into offense. What we meant as a shield becomes a club.

We feel misunderstood . . . so we strike back.

We feel dismissed . . . so we manipulate to be heard.

This session is about becoming aware of that instinct and choosing a wiser, more Christ-like response.

Lightbulb #9 asks, *When I get defensive, do I also get offensive?*

Am I wounding back because I feel wounded?

Am I justifying harshness as "honesty" or "self-protection"?

This kind of self-awareness matters. The moment I admit, "I'm reacting because I feel attacked," is the moment I can respond with humility instead of hostility.

Lightbulb #10 takes it deeper: *Am I trying to motivate or manipulate?*

We all want to be heard. We all want change. But guilt, pressure, or coldness won't create it. Meeting our spouse's deepest need for love and respect will.

This session is about humility that resists attacking, authenticity that avoids manipulation, and a commitment to influence, not control.

Let's begin.

Connect [5 TO 15 MINUTES]

Get the session started by choosing one or both of the following questions to discuss:

- Can you think of a time when your defensiveness misrepresented your heart and instead of blaming others for misunderstanding you, you chose to adjust your response? What changed as a result, and what did that moment teach you that still matters today?

— or —

- Who in your life truly motivated or influenced you to grow? What did they say or do? Why did it make such an impact? How might that shape the way one spouse motivates the other?

Watch [30 TO 40 MINUTES]

As you watch, jot down any thoughts that speak to your heart. Many key ideas are already outlined here so you can stay fully present.

Outline: Lightbulb Moments #9 & #10

I. Lightbulb Moment #9—Our Self-Awareness: When I Get Defensive, Do I Get Offensive Too?

- Scriptural Foundation
  - In Ephesians 5:33, God calls husbands to love; wives to respect.
  - Things get crazy, though, when she feels unloved and reacts disrespectfully.
  - Or, when he feels disrespected, he reacts unlovingly.
- The Crazy Cycle at Work
  - Defensiveness often lands as offensiveness.
  - We excuse our reactions as "reasonable" and see our spouse's as "ridiculous."
  - We want grace for ourselves, judgment for the other.
- Examples About What I Have Failed to Decode About My Defensiveness
  - Gets quiet → she feels abandoned
  - Raises voice → she feels overpowered
  - Walks away → she feels rejected
  - Sarcasm → she feels mocked
  - Corrects or explains too quickly → she feels dismissed
  - Brings up the past → she feels unheard
  - Eye rolls or sighs → she feels disrespected
  - Bottom Line: Our defensive stance often wounds—even when we mean well.
- Examples About What I Have Failed to Decode in Sarah's Defensiveness
  - Snapping → feels unheard
  - Silence → trying not to make it worse
  - Sarcasm → hiding shame
  - Blame → feeling powerless
  - Criticism → insecurity
  - Bringing up the past → wound hasn't healed

Key Scriptures:

- James 1:19–20: Be quick to hear, slow to speak.
- Proverbs 18:13: Don't answer before listening.
- Genesis 30:1–2: Rachel and Jacob caught in mutual defensiveness.

- A Shield Becomes a Club
  - In protecting ourselves, we often hurt our spouse.

- Who Moves First?
  - The one who sees themselves as the most mature.
  - If you think your spouse is being childish, be the adult in the room.

Real-Life Insights:

- "Her complaints weren't contempt—they were cries for connection."
- "My criticism came from pain—but it sounded like attack."

II. Lightbulb Moment #10—Our Authenticity: Motivation Without Manipulation

- The Illusion of Motivation
  - Trying to change our spouse through guilt, sarcasm, silence, or pressure doesn't work.
  - Manipulation controls. Authenticity inspires.
- The Energizing Cycle
  - His love motivates her respect. Her respect motivates his love.
  - You can't control your spouse's behavior, but you can influence it through your own.
- Common Tactics That Fail
  - Silent treatment.
  - Sarcasm or guilt.
  - Withholding affection.
  - Controlling or correcting.
  - These de-energize the relationship.
- Research Support
  - Ephesians 5:33: Love and respect are God's design.
  - Post-conference surveys show:
    - 96% of men: "Love motivates my wife."
    - 94% of women: "Respect motivates my husband."
- Unconditional Love and Respect
  - Hosea 3:1: Hosea loves Gomer despite unfaithfulness.
  - 1 Peter 3:1–2: Wives can influence husbands with respectful behavior.
  - Authenticity isn't passivity but spiritual maturity.

Practical Acronyms:

COUPLE—How a husband loves his wife:

C Closeness
O Openness
U Understanding
P Peacemaking
L Loyalty
E Esteem

CHAIRS—How a wife respects her husband:

C Conquest
H Hierarchy
A Authority
I Insight
R Relationship
S Sexuality

- Misapplied Motivation
  - She wants connection → uses criticism
  - He wants respect → demands it
  - She wants peace → shames him
  - He wants sex → withholds affection
  - Our tactics undermine our need.

Real-Life Reflections:

- *A husband*: "I stopped fixing. I just loved her, and she noticed."
- *A wife*: "Respecting him (e.g., a respectful demeanor and tone) gave me peace, even when things didn't change."

- Final Questions for Reflection
  - Are you using negative tactics to bring positive change?
  - How do your defensive reactions come across?
  - Are you willing to love or respect unconditionally?
- Takeaway
  - Authentic love and respect aren't weakness or manipulation but maturity in action.

Notes

Use this space to jot down what moved you, challenged you, or gave you fresh perspective.

Notes

Group Discussion (30 TO 45 MINUTES)

Take a few minutes to share what encouraged you—something God stirred in your heart or something you saw in yourself in a new way.

Group Reflection Prompts

1. Was there a moment in the video that made you laugh at yourself or feel understood in a fresh way? A "yes, that's me" moment?
2. Did any of the examples from my marriage with Sarah feel familiar—not in a heavy way but in a "that's us too" kind of way?
3. I said that our defensive reactions can feel offensive to the other person but we often don't see it. What helps you stay self-aware without slipping into guilt?
4. Was there a line or verse that stood out to you? Why do you think it stayed with you?
5. The image of the shield becoming a club—did that reframe any recent moment for you? Not to shame yourself, but to better understand what happened?
6. I said that love and respect energize each other and hostility and contempt do not. In other words, can you be negative to motivate your spouse to be positive?
7. What are some subtle ways you try to "motivate" your spouse that may discourage them?
8. How does the idea of "influence without control" ring true to you, even though feels like one loses power?
9. Was there a moment that made you think, *That's me*? What part brought hope or clarity to your situation?
10. Is there an area where God may be inviting you to offer love or respect—not to get a response, but simply to be faithful to Him?
11. What's one small, quiet step you sense God nudging you to take—not to change your spouse, but to reflect Christ in your marriage?

Let's Close with Encouragement

Sometimes we are moved by what others share but don't always say so. This is a moment to affirm and encourage someone in the group. No pressure, but if something blessed you, speak it out. "What encouraged me most tonight was when someone shared about this . . ."

Husband and Wife Discussion [5 TO 15 MINUTES]

Choose one or two of these statements to reflect on or share.

Conversation Starters

1. "The Crazy Cycle really helped me see how my defensive reactions can land as offensive, and how that works both ways."
2. "I was encouraged by the idea that your reactions might come from pain, not rejection of me. That helped me listen differently."
3. "There was a moment in the video when I thought, *We've actually come a long way*. That gave me hope."
4. "When Emerson said, 'Faithfulness to God is never wasted,' that stuck with me."
5. "Laughing at that *Reader's Digest* story reminded me that we need to smile together more often. That lifted my heart."
6. "When Emerson said a shield can become a club, I saw myself in that, and I want to do better."
7. "I was encouraged to remember that we're both good-willed people learning to grow."
8. "It helped to hear that God has already given me the tools to energize you, especially through love and respect."
9. "I'm walking away with this: Even my small acts of love or respect can shift the atmosphere between us."

Group Prayer [5 TO 10 MINUTES]

Close in silence or prayer. One of you may say, *"Father, thank You for helping us see ourselves more clearly and to love and respect more sincerely. Show us when our defensiveness turns offensive; not to shame us, but to shape us. Give us humility to admit when we're reacting and courage to own our part. Thank You for reminding us we don't have to manipulate to motivate—that being real matters more than being strategic, especially when control creeps in. Help us see the heart behind our spouse's reactions. Remind us that behind every defense is a need we can help meet. We won't always get it right. But thank You that we can always reset. You're patient with us, even in our messy, human moments. We trust You with the process. Thank You for how far You've already brought us. In Jesus' name. Amen."*

SESSION FIVE

PERSONAL STUDY

You began this study by exploring your core beliefs and deepening your faith. Then you moved into strengthening communication with your spouse. Now, in this final stretch, you'll grow in inner wisdom and maturity. As you go through this week's study and Scripture, ask God to reveal any ways you may lash out or try to control your spouse, often without realizing it. Keep jotting down your responses and note what personally encourages you to share during your fifteen-minute Weekly Check-In. If you're reading *Lightbulb Moments in Marriage* alongside this study, first read chapters 9–10.

LIGHTBULB MOMENT #9

WHEN I GET DEFENSIVE, DO I GET OFFENSIVE TOO?

Biblical Foundation

Ephesians 5:33

"Each one of you also must love his wife as he loves himself, and the wife must respect her husband."

Paul's command isn't just instructional; it's diagnostic. I discovered a truth hidden in plain sight in this holy text. It reveals a relational pattern common in marriage:

- When a wife feels unloved, she may defensively react in ways that feel disrespectful and offensive to her husband.
- When a husband feels disrespected, he may react in defensive ways that feel unloving and offensive to his wife.

Did the Lord know that my defensive reaction could prove offensive to my spouse? Yes, which explains why He commands husbands to love and wives to respect to prevent the Crazy Cycle.

"But Emerson," you ask, "what would give me the incentive to obey God's command to submit to my spouse's need for love and respect when I feel unloved and disrespected?"

Reverence for Jesus.

Paul frames this whole section with Ephesians 5:21: "Submit to one another out of reverence for Christ." That's the context for verse 33.

We love and respect not based on our spouse's merit but in obedience to Christ. Our defensive reactions often feel justified. But if they end up wounding our spouse, and disobeying Christ, they are neither loving nor respectful, nor worshipful. It takes humility to say, "I thought I was just reacting, but I was actually offending." Or, "Am I using their failure to justify mine?"

Love and respect aren't just marriage tools; they're acts of worship. They're vertical decisions with horizontal impact.

But if we're honest, acting in love or respect isn't always easy, especially when emotions run high. That's where our self-awareness gets tested, because what happens when we feel misunderstood . . . or dismissed . . . or hurt? That's when we tend to react instead of respond.

And that's why we now turn to James.

James 1:19–20

"Be quick to hear, slow to speak, and slow to anger, for a man's anger does not bring about the righteousness of God" (NASB).

James wrote this to believers to be self-aware, we might say.

Quick to Hear

We often reverse this in that we are quick to speak and slow to listen. When we feel unloved or disrespected, we tend to defend ourselves. But when we pause to truly listen, we often discover, *They weren't trying to hurt me. I misunderstood.*

James is clear: If we aren't quick to listen, we mess it up. We come in with earplugs and a bullhorn. We mute them and amplify ourselves.

Slow to Speak

This doesn't mean we avoid truth. It means we don't speak rashly or from assumption. We haven't heard enough to speak wisely. James is saying to hold our tongue until our heart and the facts are clear. When we're quick to listen, we'll naturally be slower to speak.

Slow to Anger

Not all anger is sinful, but quick, emotional anger rarely leads to righteousness. It clouds judgment and causes damage. "A man's anger does not bring about the righteousness of God" (James 1:20 NASB). If we're honest, we don't usually blow up out of righteous zeal. We blow up because we feel hurt, disrespected, or misunderstood. And that defensive anger becomes offensive behavior.

Here's one practical step. Before reacting, try saying this: "Here's what I hear you saying . . . Did I get that right?" That single practice will prevent a hundred arguments.

Case Study: Rachel and Jacob (Genesis 30:1–2)

Rachel: *"Give me children, or I'll die!"*
Jacob: *"Am I in the place of God?"*

Rachel was in anguish. She felt powerless and unseen, and expressed it as a demand. Instead of bringing her grief to God, she pushed it on Jacob. Jacob, feeling wrongly blamed and equally powerless, responded with anger and sarcasm.

What happened? Two people in pain turned defensive . . . and their defensiveness turned offensive. Rachel masked her hurt with ultimatums. Jacob masked his helplessness with irritation and anger. Rather than comforting each other, they wounded each other. And this from the couple whom Scripture presents as a romantic ideal: "Jacob served seven years to get Rachel, but they seemed like only a few days to him because of his love for her" (Genesis 29:20).

Now, the very love they once treasured was strained by self-protection. What could have been a moment of empathy became a rupture.

Reflection

- When you get defensive, do you also become offensive? If so, are you willing to see that as a lack of reverence for Christ, not just a reaction to your spouse?

- What would change if you believed that your quick reactions, especially when you feel wronged, grieve God more than they fix your spouse?

- When you feel helpless or hurt, do you lash out like Rachel and Jacob, masking your pain and helplessness with sharp words instead of sharing it vulnerably?

LIGHTBULB MOMENT #9

WHEN I GET DEFENSIVE, DO I GET OFFENSIVE TOO?

Practical Application

The Cycle

He feels disrespected, turns away.
She feels unloved, remembers that day.
He withdraws, his love goes cold.
She reacts, respect grows old.
Each defends against their pain,
But in the process, only wounds remain.
Walls rise with every fight,
Both feel wronged, both claim right.
Round and round the cycle spins,
And no one loses, yet no one wins.

Neither one meant to start a fight. But both felt hurt. Both defended. And in doing so, both offended. In my own marriage, I've learned this the hard way. When I get defensive, it's not neutral, especially when it feels like rejection to Sarah. If I expect her to "decode" my goodwill while overlooking my sharp tone or closed body language, I'm asking too much.

Let's be honest. A third party might say, "Emerson, your reaction looks unfair and unloving to Sarah." And what might I say?

- "I didn't yell!"
- "She's overreacting."
- "She started it."
- "I was just explaining myself!"

But here are the better questions: Does this ever heal anything? Does my reaction build a bridge or a wall?

Here are several gut-check questions to ask yourself:

- *Does my "explanation" sound cold or condescending?*
- *Is my silence/punishment disguised as righteousness?*
- *Does sarcasm cover my pain instead of expressing it honestly?*
- *Do I expect my spouse to decode my intent while ignoring my tone?*
- *Do I justify my reactions because "my spouse started it"?*
- *Do I give myself grace but deny it to my spouse?*
- *Am I more focused on being right than being kind?*
- *Could my spouse say, "Your defensiveness feels like rejection"?*
- *Do I ever pause and ask, "Was I offensive just now?"*
- *What would change if I assumed their hurt was real, even if I didn't mean to cause it?*

Defensiveness might feel like self-protection to you but feels like rejection to your spouse. Here's the real question: Is your shield a club in disguise?

Shield and Club Exercise

- ♦ Draw a shield. On it, write ways you protect yourself: "I withdraw," "I over-explain," "I shut down."

- ♦ Draw a club. On it, write how that defense might feel to your spouse: "They won't engage," "She's dismissing me," "He's punishing me."

That's the Crazy Cycle: Without love, she reacts disrespectfully; without respect, he reacts unlovingly. And on and on it goes . . .

Know Your Triggers

What drives your defensiveness?

- ❑ Fear of being wrong
- ❑ Fear of abandonment
- ❑ Fear of conflict
- ❑ Guilt or shame

- ❑ Past wounds
- ❑ Feeling falsely accused
- ❑ Fear of rejection
- ❑ Feeling powerless

If you checked any of the above boxes, your fear is real. But when you let fear drive offense, you cause harm. When you own it in humility, you build intimacy.

What Can You Do Instead?

- Admit fear without shame.
- Own the offense, even if unintended.
- Ask for understanding, not agreement.
- Share your fear vulnerably.
- Invite accountability.
- Pray for healing.
- Replace blame with ownership: Instead of, "You make me feel this way," try, "When this happens, I tend to react poorly, and I want to grow."

Bonus Questions

- ♦ Has your self-awareness ever healed a relationship tension?
- ♦ Could your spouse's lashing out be a cry for connection?
- ♦ What helps you both reset after tension?
- ♦ Have you considered that faithfulness to God is never wasted—even when your spouse doesn't see it?
- ♦ Can you be right but also unrighteous? How?

LIGHTBULB MOMENT #10

MOTIVATION WITHOUT MANIPULATION

Biblical Foundation

We sometimes try to "motivate" our spouse through sarcasm, guilt, silence, or control—hoping it will prompt change. But that's an illusion. Unholy means can't produce holy ends. Manipulation might create momentary compliance but it slowly erodes intimacy and trust. Only authentic love and respect, freely given, can truly energize a marriage.

Hebrews 10:24 reminds us: "Let us consider how we may spur one another on toward love and good deeds." God created us with the ability to influence, not control, our spouse through love and respect. When we meet their deepest God-given need, they are most likely to respond.

Ephesians 5:33

"Each one of you also must love his wife as he loves himself, and the wife must respect her husband."

This verse captures the heartbeat of the **Energizing Cycle**: His love motivates her respect; her respect motivates his love.

The opposite is also true. When love or respect is withheld, the Crazy Cycle spins. While we can't force change, we can choose to obey God regardless of our spouse's behavior.

- A wife feels secure when she's loved unconditionally.
- A husband feels affirmed when he's respected, even when imperfect.

This kind of love and respect is not earned; it's a gift. It's a decision to reflect Christ, not a reaction to how we feel treated. Let's look at how Scripture anchors this.

Hosea 3:1

"The LORD said to me, 'Go, show your love to your wife again, though she is loved by another man and is an adulteress. Love her as the LORD loves the Israelites, though they turn to other gods and love the sacred raisin cakes.'"

Love even when it's not reciprocated. God told Hosea, "Go, show your love to your wife again," even after she had betrayed him. Hosea's obedience reflected God's faithful love to His people. This wasn't weakness; it was strength. We're not called to enable sin but to obey God by choosing love even when it's hard. Whether Gomer changed or not, Hosea's love was not wasted.

1 Peter 3:1–2

"Wives, in the same way submit yourselves to your own husbands so that, if any of them do not believe the word, they may be won over without words by the behavior of their wives, when they see the purity and reverence of your lives."

Win without a word. Peter calls wives to win over their disobedient husbands not through arguments but through the "purity and reverence" of their lives. This isn't passivity; it's influence. Peter doesn't tell wives to overpower their husbands spiritually but to let their lives speak with gentle strength. Respectful presence, not disrespectful pressure, opens the heart.

COUPLE and CHAIRS: Motivating Without Manipulating

These passages remind us that we don't love or respect to manipulate a change in our spouse. We do it because Christ calls us to be loving and respectful regardless—and if anything will win a disobedient spouse, or one with flaws that need changing, this is the route. So, what does it actually look like to love or respect in everyday life? These acronyms provide the answer.

COUPLE—How to Love a Wife

(Each trait connects to her heart and reflects Christ's love.)

- **C** **Closeness** (Genesis 2:24). Be present emotionally and physically. She desires connection, not just proximity.
- **O** **Openness** (1 Peter 3:7). Share your heart. Let her in; don't shut her out.
- **U** **Understanding** (James 1:19). Listen first. Don't rush to fix—seek to understand.
- **P** **Peacemaking** (Romans 12:18). Humble yourself. Be quick to reconcile and create unity.
- **L** **Loyalty** (Malachi 2:14). Reassure her you're "all in." Speak and act with commitment.
- **E** **Esteem** (Proverbs 31:28). Celebrate her. Speak words that show she's cherished.

CHAIRS—How to Respect a Husband

(Each trait affirms his spirit and sense of honor.)

- **C** **Conquest** (Genesis 2:15). Admire his drive to provide and achieve—even when he falls short.
- **H** **Hierarchy** (Ephesians 5:23). Support his God-given role of responsibility—not as superiority, but as protective leadership.

- **A** **Authority** (1 Corinthians 11:3; Colossians 3:18; 1 Timothy 2:12). Trust his spiritual accountability to God and let him feel you believe in his responsibility.
- **I** **Insight** (1 Peter 3:7). Appreciate his counsel and input. Don't dismiss or override his voice reflexively.
- **R** **Relationship** (Titus 2:4). Be his friend. Engage shoulder-to-shoulder—join him in what he enjoys.
- **S** **Sexuality** (1 Corinthians 7:5). Affirm his God-given sexual need. This connection often opens emotional intimacy.

Reflection

- ♦ Which of these traits most motivates your spouse?
- ♦ Which one could you grow in?
- ♦ What small step could you take this week to energize your spouse—without conditions?

Key Thought

Unconditional love and respect don't mean passivity or perfection—they mean obedience to Christ. You don't need to be flawless, just faithful. God honors even your smallest step of obedience. **You can do this.**

LIGHTBULB MOMENT #10

MOTIVATION WITHOUT MANIPULATION

Practical Application

Many of us have tried to "motivate" our spouse through sarcasm, guilt-tripping, withdrawal, or dismissiveness. We wanted connection, but what they heard was disapproval: "You're not treating me right." We may have had good intentions, but we used poor tactics.

Identify Your "Unholy Means" Inventory

Do a brief "unholy means" inventory. Ask yourself these questions:

- *Do I criticize to create closeness?*
- *Do I withhold affection hoping to get attention?*
- *Do I dismiss my spouse's efforts hoping they'll "try harder"?*
- *What is the outcome—compliance or quiet resentment?*

Replace Manipulation with Motivation

Often, we long for real love or respect from our spouse, but when it goes unmet, we drift into control tactics. Not out of cruelty, but out of pain. But here's the truth: Discomfort doesn't awaken hearts. Love and respect do.

Manipulation seeks to get a reaction. Motivation chooses to honor God regardless of the response. The Energizing Cycle (Ephesians 5:33) reminds us: His love motivates her respect; her respect motivates his love.

Ask yourself, *Am I obeying because it's right or only when I get the results I want?*

Shift your posture from control to calling:

- *I will affirm, not guilt.*
- *I will speak respectfully, not to be admired, but to honor Christ.*

Speak the "Mother Tongue"

He hears respect. She hears love. Small changes in tone make big differences:

- Wives: "I'm not trying to dishonor you."
- Husbands: "Help me say this more lovingly."

When I softened my tone with Sarah, she heard my heart, not my defensiveness. Try preemptive humility: "I may not be saying this well, but I'm not trying to be unloving or disrespectful."

Own Past Manipulation

You don't need a dramatic apology—just a sincere one. Practice integrity, not strategy.

- From a wife: "I'm sorry for times I came across as disrespectful when I felt hurt. I want to build connection, not distance. Thank you for your patience."
- From a husband: "When I've felt disrespected, I've shut down or been short. That hurt you—and I see that now. I want to love you better, with warmth and presence."

Create a Motivation Toolbox

Using COUPLE and CHAIRS, choose one small act to energize your spouse this week:

♦ For wives (respect):

- ❑ "I'll thank him for his work—out loud."
- ❑ "I'll ask what he thinks and affirm his insight."
- ❑ "I'll join him in something he enjoys."

♦ For husbands (love):

- ❑ "I'll sit with her, no phone, and really listen."
- ❑ "I'll share what's been on my mind to invite her in."
- ❑ "I'll listen without jumping in to solve."

These aren't tactics. They're acts of goodwill that speak deeply to your spouse's heart.

Declare Your Calling

♦ Write your own motivation statement: "I choose to be ____________________, even when ______________, because Christ has called me to ____________________."

You're not manipulating; you're maturing. You're not reacting; you're reflecting Christ.

Weekly Check-In

This might have been a tough week of exercises for you. It's hard to be honest with yourself, and you might feel like a failure. But remember, "though the righteous fall seven times, they rise again" (Proverbs 24:16). God will meet you where you are, so don't be afraid to get back up and try again.

Suggested Conversation Starters [PICK 2 TO 3]

Share something that encouraged you from this week's session . . .

- "I realized I've been reacting defensively, and it has probably felt offensive to you. That opened my eyes."
- "Hearing that a shield can become a club hit me. I think I've used self-protection in ways that hurt you."
- "I was moved by the idea that your negative tone is not always aggression but sometimes pain. That softened me."
- "The part about motivating through love and respect instead of manipulating really challenged me. I want to grow in that."
- "It encouraged me to hear how someone stopped trying to fix their spouse and simply started seeing them. That gave me hope."
- "I am beginning to see that small changes in how I speak or act can shift the tone between us, and that gives me something to aim for."

Looking Ahead

Read **chapters 11–12** in *Lightbulb Moments in Marriage* before the next group gathering. Use the space below to note anything that stands out, challenges you, or encourages you.

BEFORE GROUP MEETING	Read chapters 11–12 and the postscript in *Lightbulb Moments in Marriage* Read the Welcome section (page 128)
GROUP MEETING	Discuss the Connect questions (page 128) Watch the video teaching for session 6 and take notes (pages 129–131) Engage in a Group Discussion on the material (pages 131–132) Couples have a Husband and Wife Discussion (page 132) Close in Group Prayer (page 132)
PERSONAL STUDY	
LIGHTBULB MOMENT #11: BIBLICAL FOUNDATION	Complete the Biblical Foundation personal study for Lightbulb Moment #11 (pages 134–136)
LIGHTBULB MOMENT #11: PRACTICAL APPLICATION	Complete the Practical Application personal study for Lightbulb Moment #11 (pages 137–140)
LIGHTBULB MOMENT #12: BIBLICAL FOUNDATION	Complete the Biblical Foundation personal study for Lightbulb Moment #12 (pages 141–142)
LIGHTBULB MOMENT #12: PRACTICAL APPLICATION	Complete the Practical Application personal study for Lightbulb Moment #12 (pages 143–145)
WEEKLY CHECK-IN	Connect with your spouse during the week to discuss your key insights from this session (page 146)

SESSION SIX

OUR FORGIVENESS AND OUR EMPOWERMENT

LIGHTBULB #11:

Not Offending—Just Misunderstood

Often, what hurts us may not have been meant to harm us. We can first look past the offense, to their pain, then gently address true sin.

LIGHTBULB #12:

Free and Strong When I Live Out, "My Response Is My Responsibility"

As counterintuitive as it feels, inner strength and freedom grow when I embrace this: "My response is my responsibility."

Welcome [READ ON YOUR OWN]

This session explores two important truths:

- **Lightbulb #11:** Sometimes the pain we feel in marriage wasn't meant as harm but was simply a misunderstanding.
- **Lightbulb #12:** Even when we are hurt, we are not powerless, because our response is still our responsibility.

You will hear real-life examples and biblical insights about forgiveness, ownership, and freedom. The goal isn't to ignore pain but to gain clarity and reclaim peace.

As you read, reflect, and share, remember that you are not alone. Every couple wrestles with these issues in some way.

If I had my druthers, I would say to Sarah, "Honey, my response is my responsibility, and your response is your responsibility, and the sooner you get this, the happier I will be." I might also say, "Sarah, I would totally forgive you if you would just see how wrong you were about me in the first place!"

Did I hear you say, "Emerson, that is not how it works"?

But . . . may I gently say the same to you?

Ouch.

Let's walk humbly into this session with humor, honesty, and hearts open to what God wants to show us.

Connect [5 TO 15 MINUTES]

Choose one of the following questions that applies to you and briefly share with the group.

- Can you recall a time when you misunderstood someone's motive and later realized they were not trying to hurt you? What helped you see it differently?
- When has forgiveness set you free more than it changed the other person? What shifted inside you?
- Have you ever assumed offense but later realized it was more about your own pain or fear than their intent? What brought clarity?
- Who has modeled strong ownership for their words and actions in your life? How did that shape you?
- What does "My response is my responsibility" look like for you personally? Does it feel empowering, intimidating, or both?

Watch [30 TO 40 MINUTES]

As you watch, jot down any thoughts that speak to your heart. Many key ideas are already outlined here so you can stay fully present.

Outline: Lightbulb Moments #11 & #12

I. Lightbulb Moment #11—Our Forgiveness: Not Offending—Just Misunderstood

- Hurt Is Not Always Intended
  - Sometimes pain comes not from malice but from misunderstanding.
  - It is not about "spatulas." It is about assumptions that harm was intended.
- Misunderstandings Can Quickly Escalate
  - Misunderstandings often escalate into bitterness.
  - A missed cue becomes a personal offense.
  - "They meant to hurt me" becomes the narrative.
- Examples of Emotional Misreads
  - His silence felt like abandonment, but was actually restraint.
  - Her planning felt controlling, but was actually about calming anxiety.
  - A raised voice felt disrespectful or unloving, but was actually a cry for connection.
- The Consequences of Bitterness
  - Marriages usually do not break up from betrayal but from unresolved bitterness.
  - Rehearsed offenses—a snapshot mistaken for the full story.

Four Relinquishments That Lead to Forgiveness:

1. Relinquish the right to rehearse; stop replaying.
2. Relinquish the right to resent, stop feeding the fire.
3. Relinquish the right to revile, stop sarcastic attacks.
4. Relinquish the right to retaliate, stop punishing your spouse emotionally.

- What Forgiveness Does
  - Forgiveness does not erase the past; it releases its power over you.
  - Key verse: "When he was reviled, he did not revile in return . . . but continued entrusting himself to him who judges justly" (1 Peter 2:23 ESV).

II. Lightbulb Moment #12—Our Empowerment: "My Response Is My Responsibility"

- The Core Insight
  - Speck of sand in an eye versus in an oyster.

  - Same irritant, but different outcome.
  - Marriage reveals who you are; it does not make you that way.
- Your Freedom
  - You are free to choose your response.
  - You are not a victim of your spouse's behavior.
  - Bitterness is a prison you voluntarily enter.
- Rose or Skunk
  - Pressure reveals internal fragrance or funk.
  - What is *inside* of you is what comes *out*.
- Misplaced Blame in Marriage
  - "My spouse made me do it" vs. "My reaction is my choice."
  - Your spouse reveals you; they do not define you.
- Reacting to Emotions
  - Jesus felt deeply but never sinned.
  - Emotions are real but not always right.
  - Do not let sadness become self-pity or frustration become contempt.
- Your Inner Sanctuary
  - Your inner sanctuary belongs to Christ. Your spouse cannot access that sacred space.
  - Responses are formed in the presence of God, not in reaction to your spouse.
  - Key verse: "For from within, out of the heart of man . . ." (Mark 7:21 ESV).

Closing Takeaways:

- When sinful emotion leads, love and respect leave.
- We are called to reflect Christ, even when our spouse does not.

Notes

Use this space to jot down what moved you, challenged you, or gave you fresh perspective.

Group Discussion [30 TO 45 MINUTES]

Use the following questions to spark honest and grace-filled conversation. Remember, these are not meant to rush through—but to open the door to insight, healing, and growth. Choose the questions that best fit your group's dynamic and time.

Reflect on Understanding Misunderstanding (Lightbulb Moment #11)

1. Can you think of a time when a misunderstanding—rather than malice—led to hurt in your marriage or another relationship? What helped you see it differently?
2. I said, "What hurts us may not have been meant to harm us." How does that shift the way you think about forgiveness?
3. Which of the Four Relinquishments—Rehearse, Resent, Revile, Retaliate—stood out to you the most, and why? Which one is hardest to surrender in your own heart? Which one have you seen bring the most healing when practiced?

Reflect on Empowerment (Lightbulb Moment #12)

4. What does the phrase "My response is my responsibility" stir up in you—resistance, hope, challenge, freedom? Why?
5. I shared the example: "Marriage doesn't *cause* me to be the way I am; it *reveals* the way I am." How does this challenge the way we normally assign blame?
6. How do you relate to the imagery of the rose vs. the skunk, the butter vs. the clay, or the oyster vs. the eye? What kind of "response" is being revealed in you lately?

Connect to Scripture

7. Read 1 Peter 2:23. Jesus entrusted Himself to Him who judges justly. What does it look like to "entrust" yourself to God when misunderstood?
8. Read Mark 7:21. "From within . . ." How do you balance being honest about your emotions without letting them lead to unloving or disrespectful responses?

Husband and Wife Discussion [5 TO 15 MINUTES]

Privately talk together about what encouraged you, what resonated, and where you are growing in personal responsibility and forgiveness. Take a few minutes as a couple, right there in the room, to quietly connect. Reflect on what stood out to you from Lightbulb Moments #11 and #12. Use these questions to guide your discussion.

Conversation Starters

1. What was one story or insight that genuinely encouraged or challenged you?
2. Where do you see yourself growing in personal responsibility or forgiveness?

Do not try to fix anything right now. This is a moment to reflect, not resolve. Lean into connection, not correction. End your time by sharing one affirmation: "Something I admire about you is . . ." or "I am thankful for . . ."

Group Prayer [5 TO 10 MINUTES]

Close in silence or prayer. One of you may say, *"Heavenly Father, thank You for Your mercy, patience, and constant forgiveness. You never hold our sins against us, and we want to reflect that same grace in our marriage.*

Lord, open our eyes when we're in the middle of conflict. Help us see what's really going on—beyond the irritation, the misunderstanding, or the silence. Give us clarity when we're tempted to assume the worst. Teach us to pause instead of pounce.

Holy Spirit, we invite You to search our hearts. If there's any resentment or bitterness hiding beneath the surface, bring it to light. Help us to release it—not because the other person always deserves it, but because You've forgiven us.

And Father, give us patience. When emotions rise, help us step back instead of striking out. Teach us to respond the way You would want us to—not react in anger, fear, or defensiveness.

We commit to grow in forgiveness and personal responsibility, and we trust You to guide us in that process. In Jesus' name. Amen."

SESSION SIX

PERSONAL STUDY

You have come to the end of what hopefully has been an illuminating and paradigm-shifting study. In this final section, the focus will be on forgiveness and how you can look past the offense your spouse commits to see their pain. You will then look at practical ways—again by mining the riches found in God's Word—for how you can be empowered to take responsibility for your responses and glorify God through them. Continue to write down your responses so you will have some notes ready for when you meet with your spouse. If you are reading *Lightbulb Moments in Marriage* alongside this study, first read chapters 11–12 of the book.

LIGHTBULB MOMENT #11

NOT OFFENDING—JUST MISUNDERSTOOD

Biblical Foundation

Forgiveness is hard, especially when you have been hurt. And it's hard to know how to forgive when the other person does not seem sorry or when you are not sure the hurt was intentional. Many of us carry emotional bruises from moments that felt personal, even if they were not meant that way. That tension makes forgiveness complicated. You want to release it, yet something says, "They do not deserve that. They still do not understand how they hurt me."

Lightbulb Moment #11 offers a freeing shift. Sometimes what hurt us was not meant to harm us at all but was simply a misunderstanding. Still, misunderstandings feel sharp and personal, and many couples accumulate hurt not from betrayal but from unclear intent.

In marriage, this happens more often than we realize. One spouse acts with good intentions, but the other feels disrespected or unloved. No one meant harm, yet hurt occurred and bitterness can follow. This is why forgiveness in the gray zones of marriage requires humility and openness to the possibility that things may not have meant what they felt like.

There may be pain behind your spouse's behavior. They are human, not hostile. This does not mean you pretend nothing happened, just that you are willing to ask, "Is it possible I misunderstood what they meant?"

That one question softens the soil where forgiveness grows.

1 Peter 2:23

"When they hurled their insults at him, he did not retaliate; when he suffered, he made no threats. Instead, he entrusted himself to him who judges justly."

Jesus responded to unjust suffering without retaliation, entrusting Himself to the One who judges justly. Peter's point is that forgiveness does not deny justice; it releases justice to God. The Greek indicates ongoing action, meaning Jesus continually placed His mistreatment into the Father's hands. This becomes a model for marriage: Instead of lashing out, we forgive by trusting God with what feels unfair.

Hebrews 12:15

"See to it that no one falls short of the grace of God and that no bitter root grows up to cause trouble and defile many."

This verse warns against letting bitterness take root. Bitterness spreads and affects everyone around it. The phrase "bitter root" echoes Deuteronomy 29:18 and warns that unresolved hurt can poison a marriage and home. Forgiveness uproots what would otherwise become destructive.

Proverbs 24:16

"For though the righteous fall seven times, they rise again, but the wicked stumble when calamity strikes."

The righteous fall repeatedly but keep rising. The point is not perfection but resilience. In marriage, even after failing to forgive or after conflict, we get up again with humility and grace.

Ephesians 4:26

" 'In your anger do not sin': Do not let the sun go down while you are still angry."

Paul does not condemn anger itself, but lingering anger leads to sin and gives the enemy a foothold. Paul is calling couples to deal with emotions in a timely, healthy way.

Summary

Together, these verses offer a framework for forgiveness:

- 1 Peter 2:23 → Entrust justice to God
- Hebrews 12:15 → Guard against bitterness
- Proverbs 24:16 → Rise again after failures
- Ephesians 4:26 → Address anger before it settles

Reflection Questions

♦ When you feel misunderstood or mistreated, what does entrusting yourself to God look like practically?

- Do you sense any roots of bitterness growing? What would uprooting them involve this week?

- What is one way you can rise again after a recent misstep in your marriage?

- How do you recognize when anger is becoming a foothold for the enemy? How can you respond biblically?

When we remember that forgiveness is not excusing an offense but freeing the heart, we can reflect Christ's love even in the difficult moments of misunderstanding.

LIGHTBULB MOMENT #11

NOT OFFENDING—JUST MISUNDERSTOOD

Practical Application

These exercises flow from what God has had to teach me—from my own misunderstandings, hurt moments, and the forgiveness I've had to extend in my life. My hope is that this helps you move from pain to peace, from offense to understanding, and from resentment to release.

How Easily Do You Hold On to Bitterness?

- On a scale of 1 to 10, how often do you hold on to bitterness?

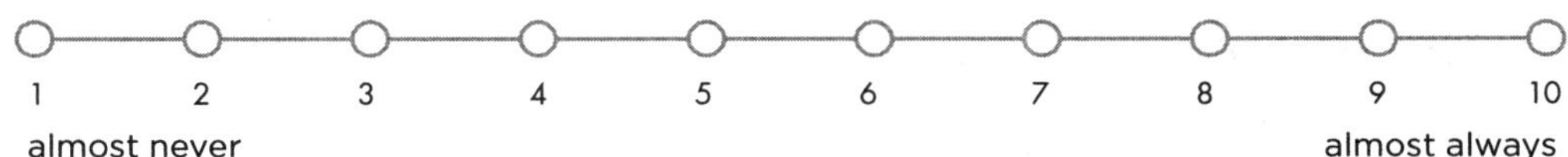

- Now think of a recent moment of offense. What did your spouse do that hurt you?

- What story did you tell yourself about your spouse's motive?

- Did you later realize it wasn't what you thought? Explain.

- How might forgiveness begin for you when you consider that moment?

What Really Causes Your Conflicts?

I laughed the first time I heard, *"Only marriage can turn a missing spatula into an act of war."* But it's true. Most of what stings us isn't sin; it's misunderstanding.

In my marriage, Sarah's raised voice can feel disrespectful to me. My silence can feel unloving to her. But why? She and I try to ask the *why* question. Otherwise, she and I know that we will not be happy with each other—and from our family of origins, we have observed how people become resentful.

Ask yourself how often each of these factors contributes to tension in your relationship:

- Misunderstanding
- Miscommunication
- Emotional defensiveness
- Fear or fatigue
- Stress
- Unmet expectations
- Personality differences

♦ How often do these show up?

♦ Do these factors enable you to be more understanding and forgiving? Why?

What Bitterness Do You Need to Release?

Bitterness nearly took root in me long before marriage. My childhood trauma, my father's actions, and decades-old wounds could have defined me. I learned firsthand that bitterness feels like self-protection, but it chains you to the past.

♦ Where is bitterness subtly surfacing in your life and marriage?

♦ What offense do you keep rehearsing internally?

♦ What do you need to relinquish so the coldness can start to thaw?

Meditate on Ephesians 4:31: "Get rid of all bitterness."

What "Rights" Do You Need to Relinquish?

In my own healing, I had to surrender four "rights" that felt justified at the time

1. Rehearsal: Replaying the Wound

I had to stop running the same painful scenes in my mind.

♦ Read Philippians 3:13–14. What memory loop do you need to stop?

2. Resentment: Feeding the Emotional Fire

I learned resentment didn't protect me; it imprisoned me.

♦ Read Ephesians 4:31. What bitterness are you justifying?

3. Reviling: Speaking with Contempt

With my dad, and later in moments with Sarah, sarcasm felt like power, but it only deepened the hurt.

♦ Read 1 Peter 2:23. Have your "honest" words ever turned into contempt?

4. Retaliation: An Eye-for-an-Eye Action to Punish

I discovered retaliation never convicted anyone; it just corrupted me.

♦ Read 1 Peter 3:9. How have you tried to make your spouse feel what you felt?

Marriage Checkpoint: Did They Really Mean to Hurt You?

In my story, so many painful moments were misunderstandings, not malice.

Answer the following questions with one specific conflict in mind.

- Was it sin on your spouse's part or simply weakness?
- Was your spouse's reaction personal or protective?
- Are you assuming goodwill in your spouse?
- Could you be misreading your spouse's motive?
- Can you see your spouse's wound behind their actions?

Sometimes the most freeing question we ever ask is, "Is it possible my spouse didn't mean it the way it felt?"

Closing Thought

My healing didn't come from reliving wounds. It came from relinquishing my right to hold on to them. I didn't deny the pain. I just stopped letting it define my future.

Bitterness may feel like a shield, but it becomes a prison. Forgiveness doesn't erase what happened, but it frees you from being ruled by it.

You can trade offense for empathy.

You can give up the right to revile or retaliate.

You can be free.

And that freedom begins with humility, honesty, and one simple, courageous question: "Is it possible they didn't mean it the way it felt?"

LIGHTBULB MOMENT #12

FREE AND STRONG WHEN I LIVE OUT, "MY RESPONSE IS MY RESPONSIBILITY"

Biblical Foundation

The core insight of Lightbulb Moment 12 is simple but life-changing: Your response to your spouse is your responsibility. At first, that idea may feel unsettling. You may fear it excuses bad behavior or removes accountability. But lived out biblically, this truth is actually freeing and empowering.

Taking responsibility for your response does not deny your spouse's actions. It simply means they cannot control your spirit, your choices, or your obedience to Christ. No one can make you sin. Your spouse cannot force you to say, feel, or do anything. In Christ, you are free to respond in a way that honors God regardless of how your spouse behaves.

Your emotions are real, including grief, disappointment, sorrow, and frustration. God designed you to feel deeply. But emotions are not commands. What you do with those emotions determines whether your response draws you closer to Christ or further from Him. When you feel attacked, you can choose a different path: seeing your God-given worth, recognizing you and your spouse are on the same team, looking for their pain, remembering there are different shades of right, and refusing to let one irritating moment define the larger story of your marriage.

You can choose love and respect, trusting that influence grows when those qualities lead the way. You can draw on the Spirit's power to honor God even when it feels one-sided. As you do, you will find yourself spending far more time in the Energizing Cycle than the Crazy Cycle. And others, including your spouse, will notice the difference. You will have a story of how God changed your heart from within.

Ephesians 4:26

"Be angry, and yet do not sin; do not let the sun go down on your anger" (NASB).

Paul reminds believers that anger is a natural human emotion. The issue is not feeling anger but sinning in it or prolonging it. Unresolved anger becomes bitterness and creates an entry point for the enemy. We cannot always control what we feel, but we can control what we do next.

Reflection

♦ What would handling your emotions in a Christ-honoring way look like instead of letting them lead your response?

2 Peter 2:19

"For by what anyone is overcome, by this he is enslaved" (NASB).

Peter describes a spiritual law: Whatever overpowers you becomes your master. If anger, fear, or resentment dominates your reactions, you are no longer free. Freedom is found not in the absence of emotion but in choosing not to be ruled by it.

Reflection

♦ Is there a pattern or emotion that has slowly begun to master you because you keep choosing it?

Mark 7:21

"For from within, out of the hearts of people, come the evil thoughts" (NASB).

Jesus teaches that sin comes from within, not from external circumstances. Your spouse may trigger your emotions, but they do not cause your sinful reactions. Your responses reveal what is already inside you.

Reflection

♦ When you respond poorly, are you willing to admit that the reaction came from within you, not from what someone else did?

Proverbs 24:16

"For a righteous person falls seven times and rises again" (NASB).

Scripture defines righteousness not as perfection but as resilience. The righteous person falls but keeps getting back up. They refuse to be defined by failure or trapped by blame.

Reflection

♦ Where do you need to rise again rather than letting past failures shape your future responses?

LIGHTBULB MOMENT #12

FREE AND STRONG WHEN I LIVE OUT, "MY RESPONSE IS MY RESPONSIBILITY"

Practical Application

If I could say this to Sarah with a smile I would: "Honey, your response is your responsibility. And my response is your responsibility." Of course that is not how marriage works, but it highlights how tempted we are to assign responsibility to the other person. The truth is far more freeing. Your spouse does not cause your response. Your response reveals your heart. That is not always easy to hear, but it is the path to freedom.

You are not powerless in marriage. Even when emotions run high, God gives you authority over your reactions. The real battleground is not your spouse's behavior but your own inner world where the Holy Spirit wants to empower you. What happens *in* you matters more than what happens *to* you.

Word Pictures

The Oyster and the Eye

A grain of sand irritates both the eye and the oyster. In the eye it creates infection. In the oyster it becomes a pearl. The sand is not the issue; it reveals the nature of what it enters. You are married to an irritant, and so is your spouse. What they do may irritate you, but your response to that irritation reveals who you are becoming in Christ.

The Sun with Butter and Clay

The same sun melts butter and hardens clay. Your spouse may bring heat into a moment, but that heat only reveals whether your heart softens or hardens. "Hot" moments do not have to create hardness. They can reveal the fruit of Christ in you.

The Rose and the Skunk

Step on a rose and fragrance comes out. Step on a skunk and the stench fills the room. The pressure does not create the scent; it exposes it. In marriage, whatever is inside of you comes out when your spouse "steps" on you. You cannot fake the fragrance. Pressure reveals character.

- What would your response to the irritating things your spouse says and does reveal about who you are becoming in Christ?

- In conflict, do you soften like butter or harden like clay?

- When your spouse steps on you, what comes out: a rose or a skunk?

Marriage Scenarios

The Silent Treatment

She withdraws after a hurtful joke. He ices her out for two days. He insists she caused his reaction. Truthfully, her hurt may have been misguided, but his retaliation was still his choice. Her behavior revealed him. It did not cause him.

The Bedtime Accusation

He says he is too tired to talk. She snaps that he does not care and then tells her friends he causes her feelings of disrespect. His "no" was not unloving. Her reaction was her responsibility. His answer merely revealed what was going on inside of her.

The Parenting Clash

She corrects him in front of their child. It stings. He explodes. But his raised voice was not caused by her timing. It was chosen by him.

The Holiday Argument

He prefers staying home for Christmas. She reacts as if he rejected her family. She had rehearsed the argument ahead of time—when he voiced his preference she did not *respond* but *erupted*. Her anger did not come from him. It came from her expectations and fear.

- Are you waiting for your spouse to change before taking responsibility for your response?

- Are you blaming heated moments for your reactions on your spouse instead of asking what the heat is revealing in you?

- When frustrated, do you pause and ask what is happening inside you before you speak?

- Which of your recent words or actions lacked dignity and self-control?

- Have you rehearsed arguments in advance, setting your spouse up to fail and justifying your reaction?

- When was the last time you took full ownership of your response even when you felt provoked?

Closing Thought

So, what does this mean for you? Your spouse may stir things in you, but they do not control your reactions, your love, or your respect. You are not a victim of their emotions or your own impulses. Your pain is real and your emotions matter, but *your response is your responsibility.* God does not demand perfection, only the willingness to rise again and respond in a way that reflects His heart rather than your hurt.

Weekly Check-In

As you close out *Lightbulb Moments in Marriage*, this is your chance as a couple to press pause and reflect—not just on what was taught but also on what's been changing in you. God has been gently illuminating your hearts, one moment at a time. These final questions are designed to help you celebrate growth, deepen grace, and step into the next season of your marriage with joy. So sit down. Slow down. Look each other in the eyes. And let this be a sacred space to reconnect.

Suggested Questions [PICK 2 TO 3]

Lightbulb Moment #11: Not Offending—Just Misunderstood

- How has your understanding of forgiveness changed by first asking if there is an honest misunderstanding?
- What offense did you find that you keep rehearsing internally, and what have you begun to do to relinquish it?

Lightbulb Moment #12: "My Response Is My Responsibility"

- Which word picture spoke the most to you: The Oyster and the Eye? The Sun with Butter and Clay? The Rose and the Skunk? Why?
- Which marriage scenario resonated the most with you: The Silent Treatment? The Bedtime Accusation? The Parenting Clash? The Holiday Argument? Why?

Closing Reflections

- Which Lightbulb Moment has become a part of your thinking the most? (For example, "Not Wrong, Just Different Shades of Right" or "Don't Let the 20% Define the 80%").
- What would it look like to make the fifteen-minute Weekly Check-In a regular rhythm in your relationship? (If it has proven valuable, stay with it for another six weeks and re-evaluate if it remains uplifting for you.)
- Close by sharing one sentence of affirmation with your spouse: "Something I see in you that I'm deeply grateful for is . . ."

Remember that the God who *began* this good work in you will be faithful to *complete* it. His desire is for you to experience success and satisfaction in your marriage.

ABOUT THE AUTHOR

Emerson Eggerichs, PhD, is an internationally known communication expert and author of the *New York Times* bestseller *Love & Respect*. Just as Dr. Eggerichs transformed millions of marital relationships with a biblical understanding of love and respect, he also turned these principles to one of the most important relationships of all in *Mother & Son: The Respect Effect*. As a communication expert, Eggerichs has also spoken to groups such as the NFL, NBA, PGA, US Navy SEALs, and members of Congress. He was the senior pastor of Trinity Church in East Lansing, Michigan, for almost twenty years. Eggerichs holds a PhD in child and family ecology from Michigan State University, a BA in biblical studies from Wheaton College, an MA in communications from Wheaton College Graduate School, and an MDiv from the University of Dubuque Theological Seminary. He and his wife, Sarah, have been married since 1973 and have three adult children.